SO YOU WANT TO SOLVE
HOMELESSNESS?
START HERE

ANDREW HENING

So You Want to Solve Homelessness? Start Here
Copyright © 2022 Andrew Hening
All rights reserved.
Notice of Rights

Liability Disclaimer and FTC Notice

The purpose of this book is to provide the user with general information about the subject matter presented. This book is for entertainment purposes only. This book is not intended, nor should the user consider it, to be legal advice for a specific situation. The author, company, and publisher make no representations or warranties with respect to the accuracy, fitness, completeness, or applicability of the contents of this book. They disclaim any merchantability, fitness or warranties, whether expressed or implied. The author, company, and publisher shall in no event be held liable for any loss or other damages, including but not limited to special, incidental, consequential, or other damages. This disclaimer applies to any damages by any failure of performance, error, omission, interruption, deletion, defect, delay in operation or transmission, computer malware, communication line failure, theft or destruction or unauthorized access to, or use of record, whether for breach of contract, tort, negligence, or under any other cause of action.

By reading this book, you agree that the use of it is entirely at your own risk and that you are solely responsible for your use of the contents. The advice of a competent legal counsel (or any other professional) should be sought. The author, company, and publisher do not warrant the performance, effectiveness or applicability of any sites or references listed in this book. All references and links are for information purposes only and are not warranted for content, accuracy or any other implied or explicit purpose.

Designed by: Jennifer Ledgerwood, www.ledgerwooddesign.com

Paperback ISBN: 979-8-9862960-0-5
eBook ISBN: 979-8-9862960-1-2

This book is dedicated to all of the men, women, children, and families who are needlessly sleeping on the streets of our country every night.

CONTENTS

SO YOU WANT TO SOLVE
HOMELESSNESS?
START HERE

Introduction:
Homelessness Is Solvable

After over a decade of working to end homelessness in the San Francisco Bay Area, this is the book I wish I had read on day one.

Having provided frontline outreach in some of our nation's largest homeless encampments, managed a growing nonprofit, and served in an executive leadership role in local government, I have taken 10+ years of on-the-ground experience to attempt to answer three questions:

1. Why has homelessness gotten so bad in the United States?

2. Why have most efforts to solve it failed?

3. What actually works?

To unpack these questions, this book is broken into four parts.

In Part 1, we will come to see that homelessness is a "systemic" problem. Rather than having one singular cause, it is the result of many different intersecting, overlapping, and reinforcing socioeconomic challenges.

In Part 2, using the "systems thinking" toolkit, we will explore these various issues and, in the process, discover that we are living through a unique period of homelessness that I refer to as "The Modern Homelessness Crisis."

In Part 3, we will look at some of the ineffective ways in which local communities tend to respond to this crisis and how many of these initiatives often perpetuate homelessness.

Finally, in Part 4, we will look at strategies and solutions that actually deliver results.

Along the way, through a series of ten "insights," I hope to show you how and why my own thinking on this complex issue has shifted and evolved over the years.

So without further ado, let's get to it.

Part 1:
The Fundamental Insight

Chapter 1:
A New Way of Seeing

Homelessness is simultaneously very simple and very complex.

In 2015, Comedy Central's *The Daily Show* aired a brilliant investigative piece called "The Homeless Homed." In it, correspondent/comedian Hasan Minhaj travels to Utah to learn about an initiative in Salt Lake City to end long-term, chronic homelessness.

Lloyd Pendleton, the Director of Salt Lake City's Homeless Task Force at the time, kicks off the interview with an astounding statistic. Over a 10-year period, Salt Lake City reduced long-term homelessness by 72%.

When Minhaj asks how they did it, Pendleton responds, "We gave homes to homeless people. It's simple. You give them housing, and you end homelessness."

Minhaj proceeds to express comedic skepticism that it could actually be so easy, with the satire reinforcing Lloyd's point.

Idealism to Realism

In the summer of 2010, I packed up everything I owned and drove across the country to San Jose, CA, to pursue an opportunity with AmeriCorps VISTA (the domestic version of the PeaceCorps). I had been inspired by a volunteer event in my hometown of Richmond, VA, called Project Homeless Connect, which is basically a one-day resource fair for people experiencing homelessness.

When I arrived in San Jose to, coincidentally enough, serve as the Project Homeless Connect Coordinator for Santa Clara County (i.e., Silicon Valley), the simplicity of homelessness seemed painfully obvious to me too. People just need homes.

Despite this obvious truth, within a few short months, I began to notice a certain cynicism from colleagues who had been doing this work a lot longer than me. To them, homelessness wasn't simple at all. In fact, it was extremely challenging and complex.

Gradually, I began to develop a gnawing suspicion that if I stayed in this field long enough, I too would end up seeing bright-eyed, idealistic people such as myself as woefully naïve. And lo and behold, I did. Just three years later, I wrote the following in a local op-ed:

> Homelessness is the most complex social challenge we face. The causes are varied, the prescriptions are polarizing, and our perceptions of the issues and those experiencing them are shaped by profoundly personal worldviews.[1]

A New Way of Seeing

In 2014, I entered the MBA program at UC Berkeley. At that time, I was managing a branch of a growing nonprofit in Marin County, CA (the community immediately north of the Golden Gate Bridge). Our program helped people experiencing homelessness find employment, and my dream was to start a clean energy company that could hire our program participants, thus serving as the next stop on their career journey.

Halfway through the program, however, as is sadly customary in this line of work, I started feeling extremely burned out. We were helping dozens of people get jobs and, by extension, housing, but in the Bay Area – and the rest of California for that matter – homelessness just kept getting worse. It felt hopeless.

Coincidentally, I wasn't the only one feeling hopeless. The city in Marin where I was based, San Rafael, CA, was also starting to feel hopeless. Homelessness, especially in the downtown area, had gotten completely out of control, so the City Council created a director-level position (a peer to the Police Chief, Fire Chief, and City Attorney) to do something about it.

It had never been my intention to work in government, but after five years in direct service, the role – the "Director of Homeless Planning and Outreach" – seemed like an amazing opportunity to have a bigger impact.

At the same time I started this new job (spring 2016), I also began pushing the elective boundaries of my MBA program and enrolled in a systems thinking course called Reimagining Slums with Professor Sara Beckman.

Like homelessness, slums – the low-income, informal neighborhoods that have emerged in urban areas all across the world – are great examples of "complex systems." I didn't know anything about systems or systems thinking before this class, but it was ultimately this framework that changed everything.

As Donella Meadows puts it in the aptly titled *Thinking in Systems*:

> Hunger, poverty, environmental degradation, economic instability, unemployment, chronic disease, drug addiction, and war ... persist in spite of the analytical ability and technical brilliance that have been directed toward eradicating them. No one deliberately creates those problems, no one wants them to persist, but they persist nonetheless. That is because they are intrinsically systems problems – undesirable behaviors characteristic of the system structures that produce them.[2]

Driving Systemic Change

The only way we will ever solve homelessness is through systemic change.

In 2017, Marin County, CA, had the seventh highest per capita rate of homelessness in the *entire country*.[3] Yet from 2017 to 2019, while nearly 80% of communities in California saw increases in homelessness, Marin experienced a 28% reduction in long-term, chronic homelessness.[4]

From Marin County to Salt Lake City to dozens of other communities all across the country, there is growing proof that it is possible to end homelessness.

The ability to do so, however, requires seeing an old problem in a new way.

Chapter 2:
Systems Thinking 101

We are surrounded by systems.

Sanitation systems coordinate the pickup of trash and disposal of bodily fluids. Vast agricultural supply chains get food from farms to supermarkets to refrigerators. A classroom, a school, a school district – each setting is simultaneously an independent yet interdependent system.

Technically speaking:

> A system is a set of things – people, cells, molecules or whatever – interconnected in such a way that they produce their own pattern of behavior over time. The system may be buffeted, constricted, triggered, or driven by outside forces. But the system's response to these forces is characteristic of itself, and that response is seldom simple in the real world.[1]

To begin to better understand systems, we only need a handful of concepts.

Elements, Interconnections, and Goals

At the most basic level, we can break down any system into its elements, interconnections, and goals.

Elements are all of the actual "stuff" that make a system possible.

Imagine, for example, the game of basketball. In this system, the elements include the basic components used to play the game: players, basketball shoes, jerseys, coaches, fans, the ball, a court, the hoops, etc.

Interconnections, by comparison, are the rules, ideas, and relationships that tie the elements together. Even though we tend to spend most of our time focused on the elements in any given system (e.g., who's the latest superstar), changing interconnections is where we start to see more fundamental shifts to the system.

For example, sometimes basketball games are limited to three-on-three or one-on-one. With fewer teammates, gameplay is fundamentally shifted.

We could even imagine more creative changes like teams having to play with two balls on four hoops or allowing players to be physically violent with each other. Games with these changes would look very different than what we're used to, even though all of the elements are basically the same.

Finally, we have a system's goal or outcome. Basketball's current goal is for two teams to compete and for one team to win. That seems completely obvious to us. In fact, it's so obvious it's probably hard to imagine another version of the game.

However, imagine that the goal of basketball ("winning") was to get the loudest cheers possible from fans. What would that new game look like? Team owners might start paying loud fans to come to games instead of paying for talented players. The loudest cheers might be generated not from scoring points but from fights and injuries, thus changing the rules and expectations for how players are supposed to interact.

If this doesn't even sound like basketball anymore, that's the point. When a system's goals shift, then the system itself fundamentally changes.

In practice, it is important to pay attention to a system's intended or stated goals versus what the system actually produces. These real-world outcomes more accurately reflect the true, functional purpose of the system.

For example, some systems have a clear goal and they produce their intended outcome, such as the plumbing systems in our homes delivering water to our faucets.

Other systems have a clear goal, but they do not produce their intended outcome, such as a country investing in its military to keep the nation safe but that investment provoking suspicion and conflict with its neighbors.

Finally, some systems were never intended, yet they persist in producing a predictable outcome. For example, when state governments shut down mental health hospitals, no one intended for mentally ill persons to end up homeless and incarcerated, but that's what happened.

Stocks, Flows, and Feedback Loops

Systems thinking is about finding long-term patterns of behavior. To help with that, systems thinkers often identify special elements and interconnections called stocks, flows, and feedback loops.

Returning to *Thinking in Systems*:

> A stock is the foundation of any system. Stocks are the elements in the system that you can see, feel, count, or measure at any given time. A system stock is just what it sounds like: a store, a quantity, an accumulation of material or information that has built up over time. It may be the water in a bathtub, a population, the books in a bookstore, the wood in a tree, the money in the bank, your own self-confidence. A stock does not have to be physical. Your reserve of good will for others or your supply of hope that the world can be better are both stocks.
>
> Stocks change over time through the actions of a flow. Flows are filling and draining, births and deaths, purchases and sales, growth and decay, deposits and withdrawals, successes and failures. A stock, then, is the present memory of the history of changing flows within a system. If you understand the dynamics of stocks and flows – their behavior over time – you understand a good deal about the behavior of complex systems.[2]

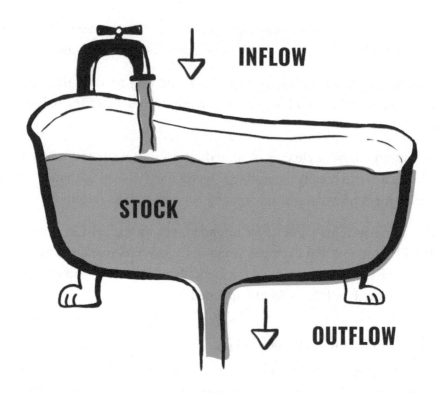

In many systems, stocks and flows feel consistent over time. This consistency is not an accident:

> If you see a behavior that persists over time, there is likely a mechanism creating that consistent behavior. That mechanism operates through a feedback loop. It is the consistent behavior pattern over a long period of time that is the first hint of the existence of a feedback loop.[3]

Feedback loops are special interconnections that regulate inflows and outflows.

When the water in the bathtub gets too cold, our nerves tell us we're cold and we reach for the hot water knob. In other words, the complex system that is the human body wants to remain at 98 degrees, and our nervous system provides feedback to our brains to direct action to maintain that goal.

Another way of thinking about this is to imagine our body's energy level. During the day we want to be alert and present. That is our ideal state of being. Unfortunately, when we wake up in the morning, we often feel sleepy and groggy. This feeling prompts action – like exercising, going back to sleep, or making coffee. These inflows ideally pump us up with more energy.

But just like a bathtub can overflow with more and more water, it's not always good to have more energy. Have you ever had too many cups of coffee? When we start feeling uncomfortable, jittery, and anxious from too much caffeine, our bodies tell us we now have too much energy and to stop the current action.

Of course, no matter how caffeinated we might become, throughout the day we will use up our stock of energy. As we do, eventually we start to feel sleepy and groggy again, and it's at that point that we might actually consider grabbing another cup of coffee.

When it comes to feedback loops, I've found it's extremely helpful to actually draw out the cycle. To do so, simply list out the steps in the process, and if it's truly a feedback loop, at some point the process will double back on itself and become circular.

With our energy level example, the process is fairly straightforward: feel tired, consume energy, stop when there's too much energy, deplete energy, repeat.

With these basic systems concepts, we can now begin to unpack what's driving homelessness in our country.

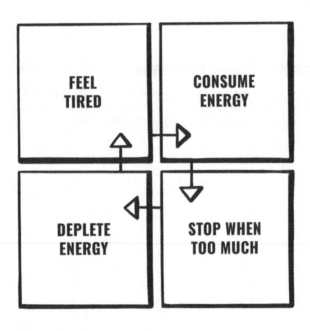

Chapter 3:
37 Days

In applying systems thinking to homelessness, the most important concept is distinguishing between stocks and flows. The failure to do so is one of the biggest reasons our country has failed to end our current homelessness crisis.

INSIGHT #1	The essential starting point to understanding homelessness is to see it as a flow.

The Point-in-Time Census

To understand the state of homelessness across the county, the federal Department of Housing and Urban Development (HUD) requires communities to conduct a "Point-in-Time" (PIT) census count of people experiencing homelessness. This is done every other year at the end of January.

The PIT – and its shortcomings – are a critical part of our story, so it's worth unpacking the methodology in a bit more detail. There are a variety of approaches to conducting a PIT, but the general process is typically something like:

1. **Emergency Shelter Count**

   HUD chose January for the PIT because it's really cold. Because it is really cold, emergency shelters are likely to have their highest utilization rates. Therefore, on the day of the PIT, most communities start by counting everyone in their shelter system.

2. **Unsheltered Street Count**

   Next, similar to the regular US census, teams of service providers, volunteers, and "homeless guides" are deployed as enumerators across designated census tracts covering an entire community. These teams are tasked with counting every person experiencing homelessness that they can find.

   HUD defines "literal" homelessness as "an individual or family who lacks a fixed, regular, and adequate nighttime residence."[1] Thus, the PIT enumerators are looking for people living on the street, in parks, in encampments, in abandoned buildings, in libraries or other public spaces, and in vehicles (cars, RVs, boats).

   To avoid double-counting, PITs are usually done at dawn or dusk when people are sleeping and/or are already in shelter.

3. **Demographics**

   Lastly, either during the PIT count itself or in a follow up effort, enumerators gather demographic information about the homeless community. HUD requires some basic information such as gender, ethnicity, age ranges, family size, and veteran status.

Communities are also free to collect other information. For example, in Marin County, the 2019 PIT helped us learn that:

- 50% of respondents indicated that the primary cause of their homelessness was economic (e.g., job loss, eviction).[2] The next biggest category, which comprised 30% of respondents, was a breakdown in personal relationships.[3]

- For people who had been homeless for more than a year, 68% reported having two or more disabling conditions.[4]

- 73% of people reported that they were living in Marin County *before* they became homeless.[5]

- 34% of respondents had some employment income.[6]

- 14% of respondents had previously been in the foster care system.[7]

- 92% of respondents said they would like affordable permanent housing if it was available.[8]

Precariously Housed

Importantly, the HUD definition of homelessness creates an interesting loophole.

Enumerators are tasked with counting people who are "literally homeless" on the street or in shelters. They do NOT count people who are precariously housed, such as people who are:

- Couch-surfing (i.e., sleeping on a friend or family member's couch)

- Normally homeless but are in jail, in the hospital, or staying in a hotel or motel that particular day

- Living in overcrowded housing (i.e., multiple families sharing a housing unit)

For the same reason emergency shelters are likely to be at peak utilization in January, "couch-surfing" and other alternative housing arrangements are also likely to be higher in January.

A Perennial Undercount

To understand the implications of this methodology, let's imagine how the PIT might play out in the fictional city of Washingtonville. With this basic example, we can see the difficulty of getting an accurate count even in a small community.

- Washingtonville has one emergency shelter with 100 beds. On the morning of the PIT, 90 people are sleeping in the shelter. (90 counted)

- Before people sleeping in the shelter are released that day, community volunteers are sent out to Washingtonville's five census tracts. Group A finds 10 people, Group B finds 20 people, Group C finds 50 people, Group D finds 130 people, and Group E finds 0 people. (210 counted)

- During this same morning, unbeknownst to the PIT volunteers, 25 people were couch-surfing, 50 unsheltered people were too hidden for the volunteers to find, 75 people who would otherwise be homeless were in jail or at the hospital, and 150 people were living in overcrowded housing with other people. (300 not counted)

In this example, a total of 600 people are homeless or precariously housed in Washingtonville. However, the community would only report to HUD that there were 300 people experiencing homelessness the morning of the count – a 50% undercount.

In practice, the true scale of the PIT's undercount, by definition, is hard to know. Studies have shown that enumerators fail to identify "plants" (i.e., researchers posing as people experiencing homelessness) up to 40% of the time.[9]

In some communities, if people who were in jail and hospitals the day of the count but who would have otherwise been homeless were identified, the PIT could be 25-60% higher.[10]

Overcrowded housing might be the hardest estimate of all. When I worked in San Rafael, CA, in the mid-2010s, approximately 50% of the city's 22,000 households were renters, and roughly 10% of renter households were overcrowded (defined as having more than 1.01 persons per room).[11] The 2015 PIT Count identified approximately 350 people experiencing homelessness in San Rafael, which did not include the people living in 1,100 overcrowded households.[12]

Assuming there isn't a compounding effect across these various undercounts, these findings suggest that a community's real PIT could be at least 350% larger than what is reported to HUD, if not even higher.

37 Days

While the PIT has undeniable operational flaws, the deeper problem is conceptual.

As we saw in the last chapter, stocks are the elements in a system that we can see, feel, count, or measure at any given time. From a systems perspective, the PIT is a method for measuring the "stock" of people experiencing homelessness at one unique moment in time.

Compared to a stock, "flows" are the comings and goings, the entries and exits, the additions and subtractions to a system. Flows help us understand how a system behaves *over time*.

To see how flow plays out with homelessness, let's start with a very specific timeframe and a very specific subpopulation: youth homelessness in 2016.

In 2017, researchers from the University of Chicago conducted a national survey of over 26,000 people, including adults in households with youth and young adults aged 13 to 25, as well as individuals ages 18 to 25. Respondents were asked about occurrences of different types of homelessness at any point in 2016 that were either experienced by the respondents themselves or by young people in the household.

These interviews were able to tease out the "hidden" homelessness that the PIT is not able to capture, including people who are precariously housed. For example:

> After Natalie was kicked out of her home at 14, she found shelter in varied locations such as on other people's couches, in an [abandoned] house, and in a shed. Because she didn't stay on the street or in a shelter, she might not have been included in a community effort to capture the extent of youth homelessness.[13]

With this methodology, the study estimated that a staggering 4.2 million youth aged 13 to 25 experienced homelessness at some point in 2016.[14] By comparison, HUD's 2016 PIT estimated that just 45,000 youth, aged 13 to 25, experienced homelessness at any given time.[15]

To make this comparison apples to apples, we can use the undercount factor we previously calculated. If the actual PIT can be as much as 350% higher than the observed PIT, then the 2016 youth PIT could have been closer to 160,000.

With comparable numbers, we can calculate flow in the form of turnover (i.e., how quickly people became and then resolved their homelessness).

If 4.2 million youth experienced homelessness throughout the year but there were only 160,000 homeless youth at any given time, that means the population of homeless youth had to turn over 26 times throughout the year (160,000 x 26 = 4,200,000).

Consider that for a moment. If the youth homeless population turned over 26 times, that means each cohort of homeless youth could have only been homeless for an average of 14 days (365 days / 26 cohorts = 14 days per cohort).

That's incredibly fast.

Interestingly, this is not just my own back-of-the-envelope calculations or something unique to young people.

In a study dating back to the 1990s in New York City, researchers found that:

- On any one day, 0.1% of the population of New York City was experiencing homelessness.

- Over the course of an entire year, 1% of the population experienced homelessness.[16]

PEOPLE EXPERIENCING HOMELESSNESS AT A GIVEN POINT IN TIME

ADDITIONAL PEOPLE WHO BECAME HOMELESS THROUGHOUT THE YEAR

In order for these numbers to work, that means New York City's homeless population was turning over ten times a year, or every 37 days.

More recent studies have surfaced a similar finding.

In Santa Clara County, CA, a study from the Economic Roundtable found that of 104,206 local homeless residents who were provided services in some capacity between 2007 and 2012, approximately 20% resolved their homelessness in one month or less.[17] Another 32% were homeless for just two to six months.[18]

It's important to note that this study only accounted for people who formally reached out to local providers for assistance. There are no doubt thousands (and I would speculate tens of thousands) of others who found themselves briefly homeless or in a precarious housing situation but did not reach out for services.

In short, by using flow, we find that, *on average*, people resolve their homelessness incredibly quickly.

INSIGHT #2	When seen as a flow, we observe that for the vast majority of people who become homeless, it is a one-time, brief experience lasting a few short weeks or months.

The Elephant in the Room

Before going any farther, we have to address the elephant in the room.

Whether you are new to working on homelessness or have been at it for years, I am willing to bet that this data doesn't match your lived experience. It certainly didn't match mine.

Over the last ten years, I have worked with people who have been unhoused for years, even decades. Many of them wear those years on their faces, in their body language, and in their general behavior.

I'm sure you have observed the same.

It's the person panhandling on the corner or the clearly mentally ill person digging for food out of public trash cans.

Based on the countless, sadly memorable experiences we have with people experiencing homelessness, it would *appear* that homelessness is a long-term, disabling experience.

Over the course of this book, we will reconcile the difference between the data and our lived experience, and it begins with a simple question – what would you do if you were about to become homeless?

Chapter 4:
What Would You Do?

In 2016, around the same time I started learning about these studies and calculations for "turnover" among people experiencing homelessness, I was introduced to Iain de Jong, who is the President and CEO of OrgCode Consulting.

Iain had come to conduct a training in Sonoma County, which is just north of Marin. As recently as 2017, Sonoma County had the third highest per capita rate of homelessness in the entire country.[1]

My colleagues in Marin who knew about Iain said he could not be missed. Based in Ontario, the internationally-recognized homelessness expert was famous for his raw delivery of hard truths that communities needed to hear if they wanted to have any hope of ending homelessness.

> Every time you make an excuse for an under-performing organization or person on your staff team, you are saying it is okay not to succeed. I don't think the people you serve think it is okay to suck. You shouldn't either.[2]

Within the first few minutes of Iain's presentation, he made this astounding claim:

> For over 70% of people who become homeless, it is a one-time, brief experience, lasting a few short weeks or months. For these people, regaining housing often requires minimal to no social service assistance.[3]

Here it was again. The incredibly rapid resolution of homelessness.

This time, however, unlike my own solitary internet research, this revelation came in a room with over 200 homeless service providers and community advocates.

As I attempted to lift my jaw from the shock of Iain's assertion, I could see others were doing the same.

Without missing a beat, Iain immediately posed a follow up question. It was simple yet profound. "If you're having trouble believing this, ask yourself this instead - what would you do if you were about to become homeless?"[4]

Resilience

What would you do if you were on the verge of becoming homeless? It's worth taking a moment to seriously consider this question.

Even if you've never personally experienced homelessness, you can imagine what would happen if you lost your housing:

- Even though your rent is really expensive, if you're on the street you're probably going to also lose your job. Then you'll really be in a difficult situation.

- If you get caught on the street with your family, the government might take your kids away from you.

- If you end up on the street, your mental and physical health, as well as any substance abuse issues, are probably going to get much worse than they potentially already are.

- And what are people going to think if they see you? Could you live with that judgment?

In the face of these possibilities, hard choices arise. You could:

- Try to borrow money or cash out your savings / retirement accounts to continue to pay your rent or mortgage. If these aren't options, maybe you try to sell or pawn off some of your possessions.

- Call any and all family members or friends who might be willing to put you up or loan you some money.

- Move to a new area to try to find better opportunities.

- Remain in a relationship with an abusive or unhealthy partner, friend, or family member.

Humans are profoundly resilient, and in the face of these challenges, the vast majority of people will do whatever it takes to remain safe and secure in their housing.

Interestingly, we might recognize this resilience in ourselves, but when it comes to other people, we often jump to "if x, then y" statements. If someone is homeless, then they must be [a drunk, an addict, a crazy person, a criminal, a bum].

According to Iain, in addition to being extremely demeaning, it's easy to find *tens of millions* of counterexamples of people exhibiting these behaviors but *not* becoming homeless.

In 2019, California's PIT identified approximately 150,000 people experiencing homelessness.[5] That's a lot of people, and as we know, many more likely fell into homelessness throughout the year. But we need to consider the broader context.

ASSUMPTION	REALITY
Homeless people are lazy and don't work hard.	In the San Francisco Bay Area, upwards of 34% of people experiencing homelessness at any given time were employed.[6]
Homeless people are just drug addicts and junkies.	About 8% of Californians (2.6 million people) met criteria for having a substance use disorder, but on any given day, only 120,000 people were receiving any type of treatment.[7] Regardless, the vast majority of people with untreated addiction issues stay housed.
Homeless people are crazy.	Approximately 20% of adults in California (4.9 million people) had some type of mental health challenge, yet only approximately 37% received any kind of treatment.[8] Regardless, the vast majority of people with untreated mental illness stay housed.

Despite our assumptions about what causes homelessness, it is often very hard to predict who actually ends up on the street.

For example, based on research from the University of California, Los Angeles, each year nearly two million people utilize public services and benefits in Los Angeles County.[9] These types of interactions might suggest someone would be more likely to experience homelessness; however, less than 2% of these County clients actually become homeless.

Intrigued by this finding, researchers reviewed millions of these records to try to come up with a more accurate way to predict homelessness. Their best projections could only identify 46% of the people who actually became homeless. Even then, their predictions were based on somewhat vague criteria, such as they tend to "be more engaged with County services," "receive County services at multiple locations," or "be in areas that are experiencing very high levels of poverty."

The Wayward Astronaut

If we can agree that most people would do everything they possibly could to avoid becoming homeless, then why do so many people still end up on the street? Iain has a helpful explanation.

Imagine you are an astronaut traveling through space. Even though it was never your intention, you find yourself hurtling toward a black hole.

How did this happen? Space agencies are famous for creating layers and layers of safety systems and backup procedures to protect their astronauts. So to be off course, would it take one catastrophe or many?

- The spaceship's radar equipment failed.

- The fuel system got damaged by space debris and isn't working properly.

- The astronaut is alone in an escape pod from a bigger ship that blew up.

- Communications with ground control are failing.

- The astronaut is mentally incapacitated from being in space for so long.

- The astronaut made a navigational mistake.

- The astronaut is now in panic/survival mode and not thinking rationally.

- There is more than one astronaut and there is conflict about what to do.

- There is infighting between departments at NASA about what to do.

As we reflect on how these different scenarios might build on each other, we can start to see parallels with homelessness.

Compounding Misfortune

There is only one commonality across every person experiencing homelessness who I've ever met – it was never just one thing.

Homelessness is almost without exception the result of a long series of setbacks, missteps, and systemic failures. Everybody is different, but sooner or later, with enough challenges, with sufficiently depleted resources, and with a diminished or nonexistent family / friend support system (i.e., social capital), the only place left to go is the street.

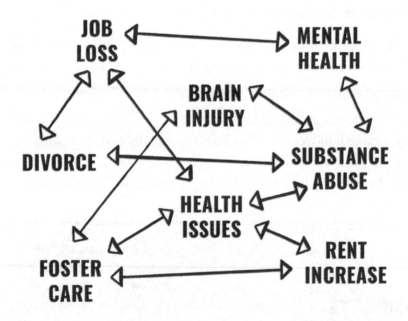

I worked with a guy named Richard who spent his entire adult life working for Comcast making a very good living, but he was laid off during the 2008 recession. Around that same time, his wife got sick with cancer. After using up a significant amount of their savings for her treatment, she passed away.

After her death, their landlord sold the house where they had been long-time renters. Rents rose considerably in the Bay Area after the recession, and Richard couldn't find another affordable option. Richard grew up on the other side of the country and no longer had any connection with that social network.

Another guy I worked with, David, first became homeless in the 1970s. During his senior year of high school, he was sitting on the back of a pickup truck when his friend quickly accelerated, causing him to fall off the tailgate. He landed on his head, resulting in a traumatic brain injury that induced a seizure disorder, short-term memory loss, and newly aggressive behavior.

His parents did the best they could to support him and keep him housed, but the physical abuse was too much for them to handle, so they kicked him out of the house. Once he was living on the street, David started experimenting with methamphetamine, which worsened his underlying issues. By the mid-2010s, David had spent nearly 40 years in and out of homelessness. He bounced among different systems of care and destroyed whatever relationships he started to build because of his traumatic brain injury.

Christy grew up without her father in the picture. Her mother did her best to provide for her, but this meant picking up and moving often. With continued moves and an inconsistent home life, she had a very difficult time focusing in school and eventually dropped out before graduation.

Christy tried to find work, but her mom eventually ended up with an abusive partner and Christy had to flee. Before she was 20, through no real fault of her own, she had already experienced multiple episodes of homelessness.

INSIGHT #3	While a crisis (e.g., a job loss, rent increase, relationship breakdown, health crisis) might catalyze an episode of homelessness, the likelihood of becoming homeless is ultimately the result of a complex interplay of other life circumstances — the broader economy, health conditions, family dynamics, neighborhood, social network.

Choice vs. Circumstances

Rarely a week goes by in this line of work that I don't hear some version of "There's no point trying to solve homelessness. It's just a choice."

If homelessness truly is a choice, then how do we reconcile the fact that the vast majority of people who "choose" to *become* homeless also decide to quickly resolve their homelessness? Sounds a little strange, right?

Kidding (and data) aside, I've never heard anything other than secondhand anecdotes to suggest homelessness is a choice. However, rather than dismissing the notion of choice, I want to reframe it within systems thinking.

In Chapter 2, I discussed how basketball players (system elements) adapt their behavior to the rules and goals of the game (system interconnections / purpose). We rarely spend a lot of time focused on the rules of the game, but they frame almost all of the decisions that players make.

Take a seemingly trivial example, again related to basketball.

In 2019, the National Collegiate Athletic Association (NCAA) announced it was moving the three-point line farther back from the basket.[10] The NCAA was open about its rationale: they wanted to make it harder to make this higher-valued shot. As a result, they thought more players would attempt dribbling and driving to the basket for dunks and other closer shots.

This might not seem like a big deal, but consider for a moment the cascading impact of a new rule (a new interconnection) like this. It affects almost every element in the system that is college basketball.

- Players begin adapting their gameplay based on their ability to make this shot from a greater distance.

- Coaches shift the strategy of how they try to win the game, including which players to start and where they are positioned.

- If more teams start relying on muscling in to try to dunk, over time, schools start recruiting and drafting different players with different skills.

- These changes at the college basketball level could end up modifying gameplay at the high school level too.

In short, the underlying "structure" of the system shapes the "choices" of the people within that system.

This applies to homelessness, as well.

People want to maintain secure housing and shelter. That's a basic human need. But they have to navigate the rules and circumstances of the broader society and economy to achieve that goal.

This isn't just an abstract musing. We can test whether this statement is true.

If broader socioeconomic factors influence the extent to which people experience homelessness, then as socioeconomic conditions change, we would expect the nature of homelessness to change too. And that is precisely what has happened over our nation's history.

Just like failing to distinguish between homelessness as a stock and homelessness as a flow, if we fail to understand the specific context of the *current* homelessness crisis, we will never be able to solve it.

Chapter 5: 1982

I was born in 1986. Millennials like me – Americans born between approximately 1980 and 1996 – have never known a United States without homelessness. Seeing mentally ill, substance-dependent people living in impoverished conditions on the streets has simply become a normalized part of our day-to-day lives, particularly for those of us living in larger metropolitan areas.

Homelessness – or the lack of a fixed, regular, and adequate nighttime residence – has, of course, existed for a very long time. One could even make the case that for 95%+ of our species' existence we were "homeless" hunter gathers wandering the wild continents of the Earth.

Of course, to equate modern homelessness to hunter gatherer tribes is ridiculous. But for that statement to be absurd, that must mean there is something distinct about the current manifestation or "flavor" of homelessness that we observe today.

Upon closer inspection, we can see that there have actually been many flavors of homelessness throughout our nation's history, each influenced by the unique socioeconomic circumstances of the time.

Colonists

When European colonizers first arrived in the Americas, they were homeless.

In fact, patterns of colonization of the Americas were in part driven by homelessness in Europe.

In *White Trash: The 400 Year Untold Story of Class in America*, Nancy Isenberg observes:

> In the profit-driven minds of well-connected men in charge of a few prominent joint-stock companies ... Here was England's opportunity to thin out its prisons and siphon off thousands; here was an outlet for the unwanted, a way to remove vagrants and beggars, to be rid of London's eyesore population. Those sent on the hazardous voyage to America who survived presented a simple purpose for imperial profiteers: to serve English interests and perish in the process.[1]

Aspirations for life, liberty, and the pursuit of happiness came later. In the beginning, Britain's American colonies were envisioned as a dumping ground for England's "surplus poor." On America's wild frontiers, it was thought that these unfortunate souls could be converted into economic assets.

Convicts were among the first wave of workers sent to the Americas. They were treated as debt slaves, obliged to repay the English commonwealth for their crimes by producing commodities for export.

For example, with the rise of tobacco farming in Virginia:

> The governor and members of his governing council pleaded with the Virginia company to send over more indentured servants and laborers, who, like slaves, were sold to the highest bidder. Indentured servants were hoarded, overworked, and their terms unfairly extended. Land was distributed unequally, resulting in further divides.[2]

As Isenberg's extensive review of primary source documents from that time revealed, there was a pervasive mentality among early colonists that some people were "entrepreneurial stewards," while others (the vast majority) were "mere occupiers."

Westward Expansion

By the dawn of the American Revolution, the economic divide was profound.

In Virginia, 10% of white men laid claim to over 50% of the colony's land, and more than 50% of white men owned no land at all.[3]

This inequality was common throughout the colonies and doesn't even account for the approximately 500,000 enslaved African Americans at that time, representing roughly 20% of the colonial population.[4]

In the ensuing decades, as America became its own country and began to grow through the acquisition of new territory (e.g., the Louisiana Purchase, the Mexican American War), westward expansion created a new opportunity for the landless and homeless. People who couldn't afford land or didn't have the connections to buy it still had to live somewhere, so they simply began living on the fringes of unsettled wilderness areas.

Established landholders typically didn't mind this arrangement. Poor whites on the frontier created a buffer between "landed interests" and Native Americans.

Once these settlers cleared frontier areas of the original people who were living there, wealthier individuals would formally acquire the land, and the again homeless and landless were pushed farther to the west.

Thus, westward expansion was simply a legacy of the British idea that poor people could be used as an inexpensive tool for colonization.

Of course, this strategy also created mass homelessness (and genocide) in the form of displacing Native Americans. Millions of people were removed from their ancestral lands during the 19th Century through a variety of deplorable tactics: forced relocation efforts like the Trail of Tears, the government's breaking of land sovereignty treaties, and the deliberate reduction of buffalo herds, which essentially starved people into moving.

Hobos and Migratory Laborers

With westward expansion finally coming to a close at the end of the 19th century, a new form of growth started sweeping the country: urbanization.

During the late 1800s and early 1900s, it became common for rootless job seekers to travel from city to city, primarily on trains, in search of new economic opportunity.

This group was far from uniform. According to research from journalist Aaron Lake Smith,

> Hobos [were] the unattached men and women traveling around looking for work; tramps the unattached penniless ones tramping around for excitement and adventure like myself, and bums, who make up the third and smallest but the most troublesome type of vagrant, the type addicted to drugs and to drink and who have lost all sense of respectability.[5]

In 1906, it is estimated that the number of tramps in the United States had reached 500,000 (about 0.6% of the nation's population at the time).[6] By 1911, the number surged to over 700,000.

Life on the road as a hobo was not easy. In addition to all the challenges related to being itinerant, poor, and far from home, hobos had to navigate the hostility of railroad security, nicknamed "bulls," who had a reputation of violence against trespassers.

Riding on a freight train without a ticket was also quite dangerous. It was easy to get trapped between cars, and one could freeze to death in bad weather. Between 1898 and 1908, the Interstate Commerce Commission recorded an estimated 48,000 tramps were killed on freight trains and an equal number were maimed.[7]

While there are some remnants of "hoboing" today (i.e., people in the homeless community who appear to be traveling or "on the road"), it's nothing like it was at the turn of the 20th century.

The Great Depression

After a decade of exponential economic growth and prosperity following World War I, the US stock market crashed in October 1929. This resulted in a panic that wiped out the financial security of millions of Americans.

Over the next several years, drops in consumer spending and investment led to steep declines in industrial output and failing companies laid off workers.

By the end of 1933, at the economy's lowest point, 15 million Americans were unemployed, nearly 30% of the country's banks had failed, home prices had fallen 67%, and about half of all residential mortgages were delinquent.[8]

In response to this widespread economic downturn, shanty towns (i.e., homeless encampments) started appearing all across the country. These areas became known as "Hoovervilles," after President Herbert Hoover, who was widely blamed for the onset of the Great Depression.

Some people who were out of work had construction skills and were able to build new, stable structures. Most people resorted to using whatever they could find to protect themselves from the elements – wood crates, cardboard, canvas, old lumber, and scrap metal.

By the end of the 1930s, thanks to the New Deal and a resurging war economy, the country started turning around, and the federal government began to implement slum clearance programs, which destroyed any remaining encampments from this era.

1982

In the mid-2010s, San Francisco Bay Area media outlets teamed up to investigate the persistent and growing challenge of homelessness in the region. If you search for "SF Homeless Project," you'll find amazing human interest stories, as well as lengthy articles detailing the evolving public policy response to homelessness in California.

What struck me most about this reporting was the timeframe. It didn't look back to the hobos at the end of the 1800s or the shantytowns during the Great Depression.

Instead, the reporting seemed to suggest that today's homelessness was a relatively recent phenomenon. Some articles even had an exact date: 1982.

To quote from a Bay Area-based National Public Radio documentary called "To Have and Have Not":

> Narrator: We are living in a time of strange economic contradictions. 12 million people are unemployed in our country, 1.3 million of them in California, more than 150,000 right here in the Bay Area. It hasn't been this bad since the Great Depression.
>
> Yet the stock market is booming. Venture capitalists are making millions of dollars over night in Silicon Valley video games. For a few, it is the best of times.

For many more, it is the worst …

… in the past the homeless of San Francisco were invisible, or rather unnoticed by those with jobs and shelter. But by last fall it was impossible to ignore the hundreds of people huddled every night in the doorways of the Tenderloin and other rundown neighborhoods.

The emergency food line at St. Anthony's has grown alarmingly, nearly 2,000 people a day come here to eat. And other emergency food, clothing and shelter charities in the Bay Area tell the same story. They're swamped.

Service Provider: We have a lot more people with emotional problems. A lot of people have been dumped out of the mental health system, literally with a handful of Thorazine, and dumped on the street.[9]

As we'll see in the coming chapters, this prologue from 1983 could have been from 2021. The situation has hardly changed, especially around two of the most significant factors described above: worsening economic inequality and a growing number of "sick" people who find themselves unsheltered in our communities.

| INSIGHT #4 | We are living through a distinct period of homelessness that began in the early 1980s. It is characterized by growing economic inequality and significant numbers of unsheltered, disabled persons. |

Part 2:
The Modern Homelessness Crisis

Chapter 6:
Mapping a Complex System

Over the last 10+ years, of the hundreds (if not thousands) of community members I have connected with in my various positions, the vast majority have had at least an intuitive sense that a worsening cost of living *and* insufficient mental health / substance abuse services are major factors spurring our country's current homelessness crisis.

Indeed, a 2020 national survey across 16 different cities found that people believed the following issues were each a factor driving homelessness:

- 75%: Drug and alcohol addiction

- 74%: Mental health issues

- 74%: Job loss / unemployment

- 66%: Personal finance problems

- 63%: Housing crisis[1]

As Donella Meadows puts it in *Thinking in Systems*:

Long before we were educated in rational analysis, we all dealt with complex systems. We are complex systems — our own bodies are magnificent examples of integrated, interconnected, self-maintaining complexity. Every person we encounter, every organization, every animal, garden, tree, and forest is a complex system. We have built up intuitively, without analysis, often without words, a practical understanding of how these systems work, and how to work with them.[2]

The beauty of systems thinking is that it gives us a practical framework for unpacking our intuition. It's as simple as starting with a pencil and a blank sheet of paper, and then applying what we learned in Chapter 2:

1. Identify all of the elements (write them down spread out on a page)

2. Draw lines between interconnected elements (add a directional flow if possible)

3. See if any interconnections (or series of interconnections) are feedback loops

4. Take a step back and analyze what these elements and interconnections are achieving

While this process is relatively straightforward, it takes time to do systems mapping well. A map should ideally undergo multiple rounds of feedback, iteration, and redrawing. The process should also include perspectives from as many different system participants as possible.

Like the old adage "measure twice, cut once," this extra upfront investment is time well spent. When we truly understand the underlying structure and root causes of a system, we find ourselves in a much better position to actually drive lasting change.

In Chapters 7 through 11, we are going to create a systems map for "The Modern Homelessness Crisis." We'll look step-by-step at issues including housing, the labor market, systemic racism, mental illness, and addiction, and each chapter will conclude with a systems map describing what we've learned so far.

If you want to jump straight to a summary of this exercise, skip ahead to Chapter 12, which will include an overview of how these different issues have intersected, overlapped, and are now reinforcing each other, thus increasing the likelihood that people will end up on the street.

Chapter 7:
Housing

As you might expect, the housing market plays a major role in the extent to which people in a given community experience homelessness.

Over the last 70 years, a series of seemingly unrelated developments in the housing market have had the cumulative effect of dramatically limiting the supply of affordable housing options in the United States.

According to Harvard University's annual State of the Nation's Housing Report, in 2019, prior to the economic fallout from the COVID-19 Pandemic, 37.1 million households were "housing cost burdened," spending 30% or more of their income on housing.[1] This represented 30.2% of all US households. Of this group, 17.6 million households (or roughly 14% of all US households) were "severely cost burdened," spending half or more of their income on housing.[2]

Suburbanization

To make sense of America's current housing market, we need to go back to the 1940s and '50s and look at the roots of suburbanization.

A suburb is an area on the edge of a large town or city where people who work in the city or town often live.

Some suburbs developed before World War II around large cities where there was rail transportation to the jobs in a city center, but in the years immediately following the war, just 23% of Americans lived in suburbs. Today, approximately 53% of Americans live in suburbs.[3]

This dramatic change to America's housing landscape was not an accident. As policymakers would learn, two things had to happen to unleash suburbia's full potential. Homes had to be:

1. Cheap

2. Easily accessible

Before World War II, homebuyers generally had to come up with over 50% of the cost of the home as a down payment.[4] For every economic class, that amount of savings was a big hurdle.

Moreover, compared to the 15- and 30-year mortgages common today, many home loans had to be repaid within 5-7 years, which meant very large monthly payments.

As part of the New Deal, President Franklin Roosevelt worked with Congress to pass the National Housing Act in 1934, which established the Federal Housing Administration (FHA). The FHA was tasked with spurring new housing development in order to support the creation of more construction jobs. To achieve this, the FHA set out to overhaul the basic business model for buying homes.

One of their most important innovations was federal mortgage insurance.

A mortgage is another word for a loan. When banks give loans, they want to make sure the borrower has the ability to repay the money that is lent. That is why banks want borrowers to have some existing savings and a stable source of income.

Mortgage insurance is amazing for a lender because it means that if the borrower cannot repay the loan, some other entity (e.g., the government) promises to cover the remaining balance.

Thanks to inventions like mortgage insurance, a wave of new buyers entered the housing market, and as WWII began drawing to a close, the government wanted to sustain the country's economic resurgence, especially in anticipation of returning veterans.

In 1944, Congress passed the Servicemen's Readjustment Act, also known as the G.I. Bill. This legislation provided a range of benefits for primarily *white* veterans, including tuition assistance, unemployment payments, low-interest loans to start businesses, and mortgage insurance.

In providing mortgage assistance to GIs, the Veterans Administration looked to the policies established by the FHA before the war, such as:

- Insuring 80% of the purchase price of a home (resulting in the 20% down payment standard that continues today)

- Creating longer loan terms, including 15-, 20-, and 30-year mortgages

Because of the GI Bill, the opportunity to buy a house was suddenly within reach for a huge number of Americans. By 1950, the Veterans Administration and the FHA were insuring half of all new mortgages.[5] By 1955, 4.3 million home loans worth $33 billion had been granted to veterans, who were responsible for buying 20% of all new homes built after the war.[6]

In an effort to meet growing housing demand, standardization became key. Developers began buying huge tracts of land and mass producing tract homes using a handful of similar architectural designs.

The quintessential example from the time is Levittown, NY. National construction firm Levitt and Sons purchased 4,000 acres of potato fields in Long Island with the plan of building the largest private housing project in American history.[7] The earliest Levittown houses were $7,000, or $29 per month with a mortgage.[8] This compared to $90 per month for a typical apartment rental in New York City. Within 10 years, 80,000 people were living in Levittown.

As William Levitt testified before Congress, "We are 100% dependent on the government. Whether this is right or wrong it is a fact."[9]

This government dependence wasn't limited to mortgage insurance.

Unlike the dense, walkable neighborhoods of cities, suburbs required new modes of transportation – specifically, the automobile. Importantly, it was another less glamorous technology that literally paved the way for wide-scale adoption of the individual motor vehicle – highways.

During World War II, General (and future President) Dwight D. Eisenhower had been thoroughly impressed by the German autobahn highway system. The Germans used this system of roads to quickly move military resources throughout the country to its multiple battlefronts.

Eisenhower wanted to make sure the US was prepared for any possible invasion effort from the Russians, so in 1956, he urged Congress to pass the Federal-Aid Highway Act, designating federal funds for the construction of an interstate highway system. When the last section of I-105 was completed in Los Angeles in 1993, taxpayers had shelled out approximately $230 billion (in 2021 dollars) for 42,795 miles of road.[10]

Thanks to new financing tools, cheaper housing options, and a more convenient way to get around, America's suburbs ballooned in the post-war era.

Single Family Homes

During my year as an AmeriCorps VISTA, I was based out of the City of San Jose's Housing Department.

San Jose, CA, is located in a large valley (hence the term "Silicon Valley") surrounded by mountains on the east, south, and west, and by the San Francisco Bay to the north. City Hall is a beautiful, 18-story building right in the middle of the valley.

During that first year, I often found myself gazing out of City Hall's floor-to-ceiling windows. I was baffled that San Jose was routinely included on top 10 lists as one of the most expensive metropolitan areas in the country. As of December 2021, the median home price in San Jose was $1.3 million.[11]

According to the laws of supply and demand, prices go up when something is scarce. What was making housing so scarce in Silicon Valley? From my vantage point at City Hall, there were vast stretches of land in every direction.

There was just one issue. All of that land was covered with seemingly identical, one-story houses.

As suburbs proliferated across the country, so too did single family zoning.

"Zoning" is the process for a community to assign allowable uses to land, such as residential, commercial, agricultural, or industrial.

For example, if land is zoned for farming, then that's all that can operate there. Similarly, if land is zoned for "single family homes," that is *legally* the only thing that can be built on that land. This means that it is *illegal* to build a duplex, triplex, or apartment building.

Single family zoning dominates our country, and it has become more common over time. In fact, as of 2019, it was illegal to build anything other than a single-family home on 75% of the residential land in many American cities.[12] Specifically:

- Los Angeles went from being zoned to accommodate 10 million people in 1960 to 4.3 million in 2010.[13]

- San Francisco's 1978 citywide downzoning (i.e., reducing zoning density from multi-family to single family) decreased the number of housing units that could be built in the city by 180,000, equivalent to more than 50% of the city's housing stock at that time.[14]

- Seattle and Portland, two cities in the Pacific Northwest with significant numbers of people experiencing homelessness, had 81% and 77% of their land off-limits to anything other than single family homes.[15]

As I would come to learn, San Jose might have had it worse than anywhere else, with 94% of residential land restricted to single family homes.[16]

6% MULTI-FAMILY HOUSING

94% SINGLE FAMILY HOUSING

Simply put, dramatically restricting what type of housing can be built is going to make homes more scarce and thus more expensive, particularly in areas with existing geographic constraints (valleys, peninsulas, coastal areas).

Slow Growth Housing Policies and NIMBYism

After two decades of rapid suburbanization following World War II, people eventually started getting sick of suburban sprawl and new policies emerged as a backlash to unchecked development.

Though I started my career in San Jose, I've spent most of my working life in Marin County. This is the community immediately north of the Golden Gate Bridge. Back in the 1960s, Marin was a national leader in the emerging environmental movement to block suburban sprawl.

To achieve conservation goals, local leaders in communities like Marin began using the power of planning laws to permanently rezone land for agricultural and park use.

This strategy was extremely effective. Today, roughly 75% of all of the land across the nine San Francisco Bay Area counties is zoned for parks, agriculture, or other rural uses.[17]

There is nothing wrong with land conservation. It is what has kept places like the Bay Area so beautiful and environmentally vibrant. The challenge is that from a socioeconomic perspective, when huge parts of the community are permanently blocked from development *and* the remaining land is limited to single family homes, the result is predictable – there is nowhere to build new housing units and housing prices keep rising.

As of December 2021, the median home price in Marin County was $1.3 million.[18]

Importantly, the pushback to suburbanization was not limited to zoning. Other well-intentioned laws have also been co-opted to prevent development.

In 1970, California lawmakers passed the California Environmental Quality Act (CEQA) in order to create an environmental review process to prevent suburban sprawl in undeveloped areas.

Have you ever heard the expression NIMBY ("not in my backyard") or BANANA ("build absolutely nothing anywhere near anything")? It has been well-intentioned laws like CEQA that have empowered opposition groups to delay, challenge, and block the creation of new housing.

Despite its original conservation goals, today, a whopping 98% of CEQA lawsuits are filed to block construction in areas that have already seen development (also known as in-fill).[19] These lawsuits contest environmental, noise, traffic, and design impacts and can be *filed anonymously at no cost.*

As we'll discuss in more detail in Chapter 9, it's also important to note that approximately 80% of these challenges are located in whiter and wealthier neighborhoods.

The Elimination of One Million SRO Units

The proliferation of suburbia has provided us with a certain conception of a home – a solitary house with a single family inside. Interestingly, "a house" was not always the basic unit of housing in this country.

The rapid urbanization at the end of the 19th and early 20th century resulted in a chaotic, churning labor force of migrants, immigrants, day workers, and traveling laborers.

According to UC Berkeley Professor Paul Groth, to meet the needs of all of these people, boarding houses, rooming houses, and flop houses, all of which rented beds by the day, week, or month, became the basic unit of housing.[20]

This arrangement was so pervasive that Professor Groth's research conservatively estimated that one-third to one-half of all urban Americans either boarded or took on boarders at some point in their life.[21]

The term "Single Room Occupancy" (SRO) originated in the 1930s to encompass this full spectrum of flexible housing.

As tens of millions of Americans left cities for housing in the suburbs, this naturally affordable form of urban housing increasingly became viewed as "poor people housing," and in the name of revitalization, cities started eliminating and redeveloping these sites.

Between the 1960s and the 1990s, a staggering one million SRO units were eliminated across the country.[22] Chicago lost 80% of its units between 1960 and 1980.[23] New York City lost 60% of its units between 1975 and 1981.[24] Denver lost nearly 70%.[25]

To put the loss of one million housing units into perspective, the national 2019 Point-in-Time Count only identified 400,000 single adults experiencing homelessness.[26]

Cuts to the Federal Affordable Housing Budget

While the federal government played a major role in shaping our country's housing market, that investment didn't last forever, particularly when it came to support for people with extremely low, fixed incomes (like seniors and people with disabilities).

Housing subsidization is often misinterpreted as "free" housing, but it's not.

The Department of Housing and Urban Development (HUD) defines housing affordability as not having to contribute more than 30% of your income to your housing costs. In the vast majority of public housing programs, people who have "subsidized housing" contribute 30% of their income. The subsidy covers the rest.

In 1973, at the same time many communities were pushing back on suburbanization, the Nixon administration issued a moratorium on almost all subsidized-housing programs.[27]

The disinvestment continued under President Reagan. In 1981, HUD's budget was approximately $32 billion.[28] By 1989, it had been slashed to less than $7 billion, a nearly 80% reduction.[29]

In real terms, HUD's budget has never rebounded from these cuts.

Rental Housing as an Investment Opportunity

Housing costs in the United States have been increasing so steadily over the last few decades that it is driving new business opportunities at both a micro and macro level.

Consider the rise of tech-facilitated "room-sharing" platforms like Airbnb. Rather than promoting communal living, these platforms have been siphoning long-term housing units off the market in place of more profitable short-term vacation rentals.

According to one study, over a three-year period in New York City, the median household looking for a new apartment was paying $384 more per year than they would have three years earlier simply because of short-term rentals taking long-term rental units off the market.[30]

In disputing the claims of this study, Airbnb made a telling admission. According to the company's own surveying, 79% of Airbnb hosts use the money they earn to be able to afford to stay in their homes.[31]

Think about this for a second: homeowners who are struggling to keep their own housing affordable are taking rental units off the market, thus making the market even more unaffordable.

This is a vicious cycle, and it's only getting worse, especially now that major Wall Street and other institutional investors are getting involved.

According to reporting from the Wall Street Journal, as of 2021, financial investment firms are now responsible for buying 20% of all homes that go on sale in this country.[32] That is up from 10% as recently as 2009.

These firms are open about the rationale for these purchases. According to Invitation Homes, one of the nation's largest rental housing ownership groups, they are seeking areas with "high rent-growth potential … [and] lower new supply."[33]

Increased Wealth vs. Higher Rents

When creating a systems map, it's important to periodically take a step back to consider what the various elements and interconnections are actually achieving.

With housing, we can now see the factors that are reducing supply and driving up prices. However, it's critical to remember that these price increases affect housing market participants differently.

If you're a homeowner, rising home prices are generally a good thing. As your home value goes up, your equity goes up and you build wealth.

This wealth can then be used in all types of ways, such as long-term retirement, refinancing to make other investments (buying another property), or even creating a financial buffer against life-changing crises that could lead to homelessness (a health crisis, divorce).

By comparison, for renters, rising rents are just higher prices. And this can create a vicious cycle where new income gains simply go toward higher rents, thus making it impossible to save for a home purchase.

In all my years of working to end homelessness, maybe 2% of the people I have met went from homeownership to homelessness, and I have never seen someone go from homelessness to purchasing a home.

When we talk about the impact of housing on homelessness in this country, we're really talking about financial burdens on renters.

Returning to the 2019 statistic at the beginning of the chapter, while 30% of all households were "housing cost burdened," 46% of renters were cost burdened.[34] The numbers were even more extreme for low-income renters, with the "housing cost burdened" designation applying to:

- More than 80% of renters earning less than $25,000

- 58% of renters earning between $25,000 and $49,999[35]

As of writing this book, it is still too early to draw broad conclusions about the impact of the COVID-19 pandemic, but early indications show that COVID's economic fallout has only exacerbated the challenges for renters. According to Harvard University's *State of the Nation's Housing 2021* report:

> Renters in general, and lowest-income renters in particular, have taken the brunt of the economic fallout from the pandemic. The Census Bureau's Household Pulse Surveys show that more than half of all renter households had lost income between March 2020 and March 2021. Not surprisingly, 17 percent were behind on rent [in early 2021], including nearly a quarter of those earning less than $25,000 and a fifth of those earning between $25,000 and $34,999.[36]

Amazingly, over roughly this same period of time, from April 2020 to the end of April 2021, nationwide home prices increased 19.1%.[37] That means if a home was valued at $500,000, in one year it increased in value by almost $100,000. To put that into perspective, the median worker in the United States earns $50,000 a year.[38]

The Housing Map

Systems thinking provides a framework for illustrating how seemingly disparate phenomena are actually interconnected. The multiple causes of constrained housing supply and rising housing prices are a perfect example.

Using everything we learned in this chapter, we can create the following systems map for our country's rental housing crisis.

We will build on this map with new information in upcoming chapters.

(Given that this book is intended for a general reader with no previous systems thinking or homelessness experience, I have deviated from traditional systems diagramming techniques in the hope of making these maps more understandable for readers. In the appendix, I have included a section called "A Technical Note on Systems Mapping" that describes the differences.)

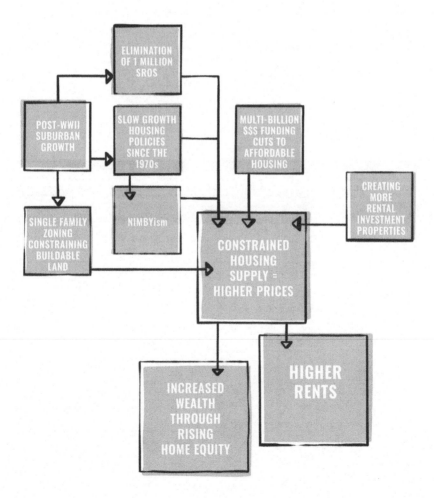

Chapter 8:
The Economy

Housing affordability is often discussed in the context of housing prices, but in reality, the affordability of something is determined both by its cost and by how much money we have to spend.

For most of us, the amount of money we have to spend is determined by our jobs. Thus, employment (who is working, how much money they're making, and how that relates to long-term wealth creation) is a critical piece of the homelessness puzzle.

Misguided Measurements

When it comes to complex systems like the labor market, it's helpful to find measurements that can indicate whether the system is performing as it should.

This sounds simple, but we screw it up all the time. One of the most common ways we do this is by confusing "outputs" (things we do, activities, programs) with "outcomes" (the intended change the outputs seek to produce).

There are countless examples of this:

- In education, we overly focus on test results (outputs), which sometimes results in high-scoring kids who don't know how to apply what they've learned to the world at large (outcome).

- With national defense, politicians focus on "defense spending" (an output) as a metric for security that does not always translate into national safety (outcome).

- With homelessness, if we focus on outputs like meals served or nights of shelter provided, we can create systems that lose sight of the fact that these activities are not actually ending homelessness (outcome).

The economy is highly politicized, so attempting to define its goals and purpose is bound to generate differing opinions. That being said, I think most Americans generally agree that:

- Everyone who can and wants to work should be able to.

- By working, you should be able to afford a decent life and not live in poverty.

- You should earn enough to be able to be self-sufficient, save, and build wealth.

To measure these goals, we tend to use measurements like the unemployment rate, GDP "growth," and stock market performance. As we'll see, however, these measures do not tell the whole story of what's happening with the economy, especially for people who are struggling financially.

SYSTEM GOAL	TYPICAL MEASUREMENT	BETTER MEASUREMENT
The Opportunity Work	The Unemployment Rate	Labor Participation
The Ability to Earn a Living Wage	GDP "Growth"	Wage Growth
Building Wealth and Security	Stock Market Performance	Savings

Labor Participation

If we want to measure "everyone who can and wants to work should be able to work," where would we start?

If you're like me, you'd probably default to the unemployment rate. It's a metric we see and hear about all the time. The unemployment rate is supposed to measure how many people are NOT working.

I never knew the exact equation for calculating the unemployment rate, so I always assumed it was something like this:

$$\frac{\text{\# OF WORKING AGE PEOPLE NOT WORKING}}{\text{\# OF WORKING AGE PEOPLE WORKING}} = \text{UNEMPLOYMENT RATE}$$

It turns out this intuition was only partially correct.

Rather than looking at every working age person (15-64), the Bureau of Labor Statistics (BLS) focuses on the "labor force" to calculate the unemployment rate. The labor force distinguishes between people who are "participating" and "not-participating" in the economy ("labor participation"). People who are considered non-participants include those who are:

- In jail

- In the military

- Sick and in long-term care facilities

- In school

- Stay-at-home parents

Very importantly though, if you are looking for work but haven't been able to find a job in 27 months, the BLS also moves you to the "not-participating" group.

So, the unemployment rate is actually calculated based on the number of people the BLS considers as participating in the labor force. A little misleading, right?

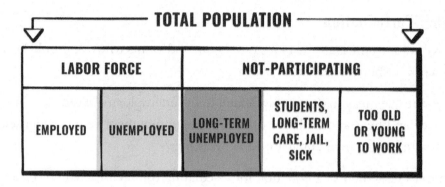

Following World War II, the US saw a steady increase in the labor participation rate. This was primarily due to more women entering the workforce (female labor participation has doubled from 30% to 60% over the last 70 years).[1]

However, labor participation peaked in the 1990s at 67.3% and has been falling ever since. As of January 2018, the labor participation rate was 62.7%.[2]

A decline of 4.6% might not sound like that big of a deal, but consider this: in January of 2018, there were 257 million Americans between the ages of 15 and 64 (the working age population).[3] If labor participation was still at its high from the 1990s, then 12 million more people would have been working.

There has been significant debate among economists about what's driving the decline in labor participation. In July of 2014, the President's Council of Economic Advisers released a report summarizing 10 of the leading studies on the topic.[4]

According to this report, at least 50% of the decline is simply due to demographics. Baby Boomers were half the labor force in the mid-1990s, so retiring Boomers have had a significant impact on the labor participation rate.

But what about the other six million people? Why aren't they working? There are three big reasons why, and they all belong on our systems map.

Unemployment Begets Unemployment

Studies repeatedly show that there is an incredibly strong bias against unemployed persons in the labor market.

For example, a 2011 study from the University of California, Los Angeles showed study participants (potential employers) resumes with the same work and educational experiences.[5] The only difference was whether the job seeker was currently employed.

Researchers found there was an immediate bias against even short-term unemployment, with study participants even rating unemployed candidates as less competent and friendly.

This bias creates a vicious, self-fulfilling feedback loop for people who are out of work. The longer they are out of work, the more critically they are judged, which then makes it even harder to secure employment again.

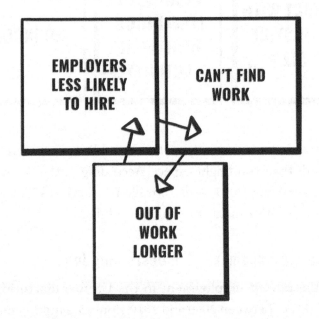

The Criminal Justice System Creates Even More Unemployment

Similar to long periods of unemployment, having a criminal record (even if someone has served their time and made amends for what they did) has a chilling effect on employers.

For example, a study in New York found that even when people had identical resumes, a drug possession conviction reduced call-backs by 50%.[6] Indeed, studies have found that over 60% of formerly incarcerated people remain unemployed a year after release.[7]

Like long-term unemployment, this phenomenon can create a feedback loop, where an inability to find legitimate work can push people back to illicit work, which then leads to recidivism back into the criminal justice system.

This might seem like a relatively isolated problem, but more people have criminal records than you might expect. According to the Federal Bureau of Investigation, as of July 2015, over 70 million Americans had some type of criminal record. That's roughly one in three adults.[8]

Technological Advancements Are Destroying Jobs

Since 1980, the rate of employment in the US manufacturing sector has declined over 50%.[9] Between 2000 and 2010 alone, 5.6 million manufacturing jobs vanished. Despite this loss of jobs, manufacturing output increased more than 150% over the same time period.

Put simply, in some parts of our economy, we are producing more than ever and we need fewer workers to do so. Technological advancements are the biggest reason why.

According to research from the global consulting firm McKinsey & Co., by 2030, "approximately 50% of current work activities are technically automatable by adopting currently demonstrated technologies."[10] In advanced countries like the US, automation will drive growth in creative, managerial, and caregiving fields, but there will be even greater downward pressure on physical labor, jobs which have historically had lower education requirements.

Looking at data from the BLS, this imbalance is already well under way:

> In 2016, the labor force participation rates for men and women with less than a high school diploma were 58.1 percent and 33.3 percent, respectively. By contrast, the rates for men and women with a professional degree were 79.9 percent and 75.1 percent, respectively.[11]

Wage Stagnation

Not having a job puts someone into a highly vulnerable financial position and makes them more susceptible to becoming homeless, but what about people who are working? How are they faring economically?

One of the most common ways to assess the economic well-being of workers is to look at the amount of money they are earning.

According to the Harvard Business Review, for wages to grow on a sustained basis, two things must happen:

1. Workers have to produce and sell more goods and services (i.e., increase "productivity").

2. Workers must then receive a consistent share of the new revenue coming from these new goods and services.[12]

The typical way to measure the growth of goods and services is to look at Gross Domestic Product (GDP). GDP is defined as "the total dollar value of all goods and services produced in an economy over a specific period of time."[13]

From 1948 to 2013, factoring in recessions and other economic downturns, GDP in the US grew 243%.[14] If this growth had been shared with workers, then we generally should have seen a 243% increase in wages. Sadly, that is not what happened.

Since the 1970s, the economy has continued to grow, but for the average worker, wages have stayed flat.[15]

INCREASING PRODUCTIVITY VS. MEDIAN COMPENSATION

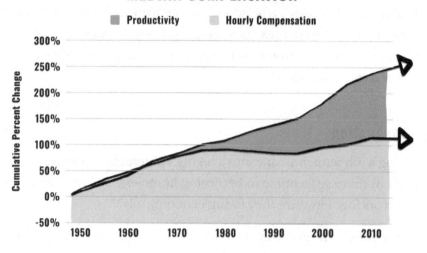

To put this trend in concrete numbers, the median full-time worker now earns about $50,000 a year.[16] *Had the fruits of the nation's economic output been shared over the past 45 years as broadly as they were from the end of World War II until the early 1970s, that worker would instead be making approximately $92,000.*

To say this in another way:

> Had the more equitable income distributions of the three decades following World War II (1945 through 1974) merely held steady, the aggregate annual income of Americans earning below the 90th percentile would have been $2.5 trillion higher in the year 2018 alone. ... [that is] enough to pay every single working American in the bottom nine deciles an additional $1,144 a month. Every month. Every single year.[17]

The cumulative impact of this is in some ways impossible to fully appreciate. From 1975 to 2018, it is estimated the total in lost wages could be as high as $47 trillion.[18]

Proliferation of Pro-Business Policies

Like homelessness, the messy truth is that wage stagnation has many different origin stories. The full breakdown is complex, but the general trend is that a series of "pro-business" policies and practices are stripping the power and earning potential of workers:

- Unions, which have used collective bargaining to secure higher wages for workers, have seen steadily declining membership. In 1954, 28.3% of all US workers were unionized. By 2003, union membership was down to 11.5%.[19]

- The minimum wage, which creates a baseline wage that employers must pay, has not kept up with the cost of living.[20]

- Companies are spending more money than ever on stock buybacks (i.e., rather than using profits to give employees raises, they use profits to buy their own stock, which increases the value of the stock for stockholders). In 2021, public companies spent a record-breaking $850 billion on buybacks.[21] That would be equivalent to giving every US household $7,100.

- Some industries are more monopolistic, meaning workers have a harder time competing for better wages.[22]

- Fewer Americans are moving to areas of economic opportunity (i.e., large cities), in part because housing has become prohibitively expensive.[23]

The result of these trends is that the share of income going to the average worker is on the decline, and the share of income going to management and owners is increasing.[24]

DISTRIBUTION OF TAXABLE INCOME

1975

66%	25%	9%

2018

50%	28%	22%

BOTTOM 90% OF EARNERS	TOP 90%-99%	TOP 1%

Wealth Creation

Growing up, we are taught to save money to safeguard ourselves against potential financial hardships, such as not being able to find work or earning insufficient income. If fewer Americans are working and those who are earn less than they used to, are savings accounts keeping people afloat?

Wealth and savings are a lot like the bathtub analogy I used earlier to explain stocks and flows. Money flows into our bank account via income. Money flows out via living expenses. The remaining balance is our savings / wealth.

Incredibly, according to data from the Federal Reserve, in 2020, 45% of American households had not set aside enough emergency or "rainy day" funding to cover three-months of expenses.[25]

In the context of homelessness, the lack of a financial cushion makes it extremely difficult to weather a rent increase, an expensive health issue, or a job loss.

Similarly, someone in rehab or receiving emergency mental health services might not be able to work and have money set aside to pay for treatment.

People who have grown up in foster care or who have a limited social network cannot easily tap the disposable income or savings of relatives or friends.

And people, typically women, fleeing domestic violence are often similarly financially limited.

In the US, we rarely see government officials and the media use personal savings as a metric for wealth and financial security. Instead, they use benchmarks like the stock market.

In January of 2021, there were 10.1 million officially unemployed Americans (curiously, 18.3 million people were collecting unemployment).[26] At the same time, the S&P 500, which tracks the value of the 500 largest publicly traded companies, was 15% higher than January of 2020.[27]

How could it be that so many people were unemployed and out of work yet the stock market continued to grow in value?

There is a simple explanation. The top 10% wealthiest households in the US own approximately 90% of all stocks.[28] Despite being used as a metric for national wealth and wellbeing, the stock market is really just an indicator of how well the wealthiest Americans are faring financially.

Economic Shocks

One of the most important takeaways from systems thinking is the importance of looking at long-term trends instead of short-term headlines.

Over the past 15 years, there have been two major economic shocks in the United States: The Great Recession and the COVID-19 Pandemic.

Rather than these events being their own standalone causes of homelessness, it is more accurate to see these downturns as exacerbating and accelerating existing economic trends.

Looking specifically at the Pandemic, which we are still living through as of the publication of this book, Harvard University economist Raj Chetty's early research found that:

> By [April 2020], one month into the pandemic, the bottom quarter of wage earners, those making less than $27,000 a year, had lost almost 11 million jobs, more than three times the number lost by the top quarter, which earn more than $60,000 annually.

> By late June the gap had widened further, even though many businesses had reopened. In fact, the segment of Americans who are paid best had recovered almost all the jobs lost since the start of the pandemic … meanwhile, the bottom half of American workers represented almost 80% of the jobs still missing.[29]

The Map

As with housing, systems thinking provides a framework for tying all of these different threads together.

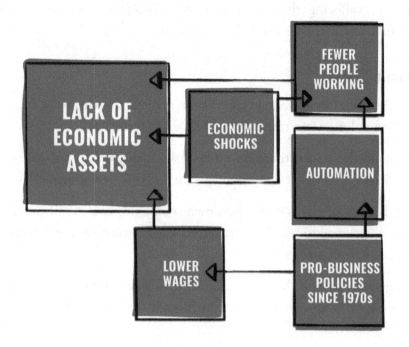

Chapter 9:
Racism

Equity is the idea that social or cultural factors (like skin color, gender, religion, etc.) should not predict success or failure in a given system. Using this definition, we can assess whether homelessness in the United States is an equitable experience.

For our analysis, we will look specifically at Black Americans.

In 2020, 61.6% of the US population was White and 12.4% was Black.[1] According to demographic data from the 2020 Point-in-Time Count, 48% of the homeless community was White while 39% of the homeless community was Black.[2]

The 300% overrepresentation of Black Americans in the homeless community is compelling evidence for the presence of an inequitable system.

When it comes to the current and lingering impact of anti-Black racism in America, there are sadly many examples to draw from, such as:

- Slavery

- The federal government reneging on reparations following the Civil War

- The violent destruction of Black property and lives during Jim Crow

- Separate but equal education policies

All of these past injustices still have an effect today; however, in this chapter I'm going to focus on two of the biggest systemic contributing factors to The Modern Homelessness Crisis: discriminatory housing and criminal justice policies.

Discrimination

Racism is prejudice, discrimination, and/or antagonism directed against someone of a different race based on the belief that one's own race is superior.

From the outset, it is critical to acknowledge that these beliefs alone are enough to bias outcomes.

In a 2013 joint study from the University of Toronto and Stanford University, researchers sent identical resumes to employers. Some resumes alluded to an Asian or Black candidate while others were "whitened" to not suggest a minority candidate (such as using European sounding names vs. names common in Asian and Black cultures). In some cases, the whitened resumes were 100% more likely to get invited for an interview.[3]

This same kind of discrimination shows up in rental housing markets. A 2020 study in Boston found that 71% of Black renters faced discrimination.[4] This included real estate brokers showing Black renters about half the number of apartments they showed to White renters. Brokers were also more likely to offer move-in incentives to prospective White renters.

Importantly, this type of discrimination alone exacerbates the already precarious housing and economic circumstances described in the last two chapters. However, the even more important insight for our analysis is what happens when -isms like racism get baked into the formal rules and practices of a system. When discrimination becomes "structural" and "systemic," it can cause profoundly detrimental and lasting disadvantages.

Redlining

As discussed in Chapter 6, the Federal Housing Administration's (FHA) creation of federal mortgage insurance was a huge factor in jumpstarting America's modern housing system. Tragically, the early implementation of that system proceeded in a way that has ultimately deprived Black Americans of access to hundreds of billions, if not trillions, of dollars of wealth.

All mortgages carry risk. If the borrower isn't financially secure, they could default on the loan. Depending on the location of a home, it could be destroyed in a flood, fire, or earthquake.

While these are understandable concerns, the FHA took "risk" one step further. In the process of developing "residential security maps" to determine which properties the government was willing to insure, FHA officials embraced discriminatory attitudes of the time.

The most desirable neighborhoods on these "risk" assessment maps were outlined in green and known as "Type A." They were typically suburbs in the outskirts of cities. They were also commonly areas with legally enforceable, race-based restrictions on who could live there.

Recall in Chapter 6, William Levitt built Levittown, a housing development that had been "100% dependent on the government." To get "Type A" designations, developers like Levitt would explicitly include contractual language in ownership documents that forbade homeowners from renting or selling to persons "other than members of the Caucasian race." This was common practice and can be found in historical housing documents across the country.

On the other end of the spectrum, "Type D" neighborhoods were outlined in red and were considered the riskiest areas to cover. These neighborhoods tended to be older districts in the center of cities, and they were also communities with the most diversity. The red markings on these maps give us the term "redlining."

In the phenomenal book *The Color of Law*, scholar Richard Rothstein found that at the beginning of the 20th century, many urban areas across the country were naturally integrating as both White and Black Americans moved to cities to be closer to jobs. However, because of discriminatory practices like redlining, many integrated neighborhoods were destroyed.

Consider the development of a 9,000-unit apartment complex on Manhattan's East Side in the 1940s by the Metropolitan Life Insurance Company:

> The process of construction began with the city condemning 18 square blocks of a racially integrated neighborhood and transferring the land to the company, which received tax relief as well. Met Life executives made it clear that Stuyvesant Town

was for "white people only" — a policy that led to protests and a compromise whereby the company agreed to lease a handful of apartments to "qualified Negro tenants," while building a "smaller development" for black renters in Harlem.[5]

After evicting Black residents from these communities, Black neighborhoods were then deliberately located next to undesirable land uses, such as industrial land (including polluting industries), liquor stores, night clubs, and houses of prostitution. A 1983 study found that there was only a 1 in 10,000 chance that the location of our country's predominantly Black neighborhoods and the location of hazardous waste facilities could have occurred randomly.[6]

Unequal Opportunity

The 1968 Fair Housing Act finally outlawed practices like redlining, but the damage had been done. Today, over 50 years later, even in our country's most "liberal" metropolitan areas, residential demographics *still* mirror the original segregation produced by redlining.

What's important about this contemporary, de facto segregation is that it helps to explain how the day-to-day experiences of people of different races can vary so wildly.

Think about it – housing is the foundation of our lives. Where we live shapes our options for banking, groceries and food, parks and open space, and community amenities like libraries.

Where we live also shapes our family's socioeconomic future. It determines the quality of the schools, which in turn impacts our children's prospects for higher education, which in turn impacts future earning potential.

Finally, where we live determines the extent to which we can build wealth.

When Black Americans were denied access to homeownership in the suburbs, they were blocked from one of the most significant wealth-building engines in the American economy: suburban real estate.

As homes in America's suburbs have become increasingly valuable over the last 70 years, White Americans have been able to use that growing equity (in the financial sense) to send their kids to college, buy more property, invest in the stock market, and/or retire.

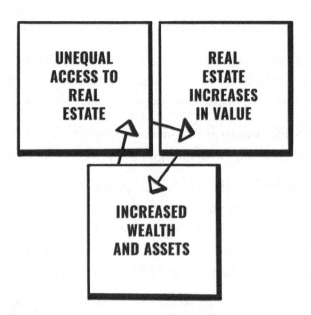

Since the Great Recession, the gap between Black and White homeownership rates in the United States has increased to its highest level in 50 years, from 28.1% in 2010 to 30.1% in 2017.[7]

This widening gap is in part due to continued predatory practices perpetrated against Black homeowners. For example, just prior to the Great Recession, 61% of Black borrowers with subprime loans (the risky, high-cost mortgages that helped fuel the housing bubble) would have qualified for conventional loans with lower interest rates.[8] This type of lending resulted in Black families disproportionately defaulting on their debts during the Great Recession.

Unsurprisingly, the racial wealth gap has also reached record levels, with the average White family now worth $171,000, or nearly ten times more than the average Black family ($17,150).[9]

Criminal Justice Involvement

In the spring of 2020, an unarmed Black man named George Floyd was suffocated by a Minneapolis police officer while being detained over suspicion of using a counterfeit $20 bill. In the wake of Mr. Floyd's murder, the term "defund the police" started gaining momentum across the country.

While "defund the police" was certainly about justice for Mr. Floyd, the fact that these cries were happening in local communities across the country signaled a much deeper, more pervasive frustration with the criminal justice system.

Policing in the United States dates back to the colonial period. As early as 1636, local community members in Boston began establishing "night watch" patrols tasked with disrupting activities like gambling and prostitution.

As the country continued to grow, cities and towns became significantly larger, and by the 1830s, publicly funded, organized police forces began to emerge.

In addition to addressing illicit behavior, police departments took on more responsibility for securing vital community assets. In the North, this meant protecting shipping and commercial centers. In the South, this meant guaranteeing the property rights of slaveholders, which entailed tracking down runaway slaves and actively monitoring for signs of revolt.

By the early 20th century, we again see new ways of using police departments:

- Business interests pushed the police to crack down on labor organizing.

- Political machines corrupted local police departments to allow political parties to skirt the law, thus reinforcing their hold on power.

- Xenophobic fears led to patrolling taverns frequented by European immigrant communities, eventually culminating in Prohibition.

From a systems perspective, there is an extremely important lesson underpinning these evolving uses of the police.

All across the country, police forces tend to be the vehicle for the larger community goal of "maintaining public safety." As a result, every time "public safety" is redefined, the nature of policing changes with it.

In terms of contemporary "public safety," much of modern policing stems from the way communities began responding to the counterculture and civil rights movements in the 1960s. According to President Nixon's aide John Ehrlichman:

> The Nixon campaign in 1968, and the Nixon White House after that, had two enemies: the antiwar left and black people. You understand what I'm saying? We knew we couldn't make it illegal to be either against the war or black, but by getting the public to associate the hippies with marijuana and blacks with heroin, and then criminalizing both heavily, we could disrupt those communities. We

could arrest their leaders, raid their homes, break up their meetings, and vilify them night after night on the evening news. Did we know we were lying about the drugs? Of course we did.[10]

From slave catchers in the antebellum South to enforcing Jim Crow segregation laws in the late 19th and early 20th centuries to the current rhetoric of "law and order," policing in the United States has always had a disproportionate impact on the Black community.

As of 2016:

- Black Americans comprised 27% of all individuals arrested in the United States – double their share of the total population.

- Black youth accounted for 15% of all U.S. children yet made up 35% of juvenile arrests.[11]

Some assume these statistics suggest some inherent criminality among Black Americans, but studies consistently show that per capita rates of criminal behavior, such as drug use, are equal among White and Black Americans.

For example, in 2010, the American Civil Liberties Union found that Blacks were 3.7 times more likely to be arrested for marijuana possession than Whites, even though their rate of marijuana usage was comparable.[12]

Importantly, using what we've learned about the interconnected dynamics of systems, we can see how the criminal justice system's disproportionate impact on the Black community has been facilitated by America's discriminatory housing policies, creating a vicious feedback loop:

- Over the last 70 years, racist housing policy has crowded Black Americans into certain communities. As we've seen, these communities tend to be poorer than Whiter communities.

- Police resources are generally concentrated in these poorer communities. This increases the likelihood of police contact with residents, who are more likely to be Black.

- As we learned in the last chapter, having a criminal record dramatically impacts a person's ability to obtain employment, thus making it even more difficult to build wealth and leave impoverished communities.

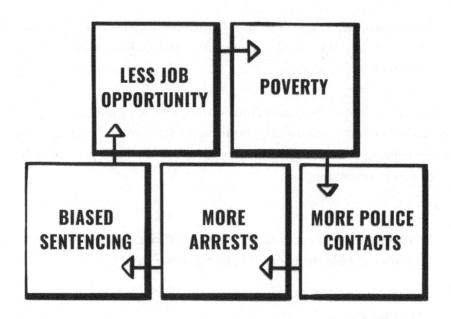

Systemic Racism

Growing up in Richmond, VA (the former capital of the Confederacy), it was common to hear people talk about self-segregation. White people lived in one part of the city while Black people lived in another because "that's what people prefer."

Similarly, if there was more policing in certain parts of the city (i.e., Black communities), that was just because there was some type of inherent criminality there.

From my perspective as a White kid growing up in the suburbs, I just accepted many of these assumptions. I had no other reference point.

I think this underscores an important insight that for many of us, it can be very hard to realize, let alone accept, that *it is possible for different people to have radically divergent lived experiences of the same system* (e.g., growing up in a certain community).

It has taken a lot of time and study to gain a better understanding of the ways in which discriminatory policies continue to shape our communities, and for me, much of this education occurred in one of the most liberal parts of the country – the San Francisco Bay Area.

Ironically, this was not because the Bay Area is so much more equitable than Virginia. Instead, it is the similarities that I continue to find so striking. How can communities without an explicit history of slavery, the Civil War, and Jim Crow have the same inequities as those parts of the country that did?

The short answer, to quote Professor Charles Payne at Duke University, is that "the whole United States is Southern."[13]

Throughout our nation's history, discriminatory policies have been embraced and adopted all across the country, and even if the views and mindsets that led to these policies are not necessarily held by contemporary people, because of present day apathy and/or unwillingness to right historical wrongs, inequities persist.

I mentioned in Chapter 2 that I was becoming increasingly burned out on homelessness. Curiously, this had nothing to do with working with people in need. To the contrary, those were some of the best days of my career.

Instead, one of the most mentally and emotionally draining aspects of this work is the hypocrisy.

People are more than happy to put a Black Lives Matter sign in their front yard or share their so-called enlightened views on social media, but when it comes to driving material change, such as approving new housing, I can't even tell you how many times I've heard "I'm progressive, but..." to preface why the proposal is such an awful idea.

This opposition, particularly in America's most "liberal" metropolitan areas, to righting the policy wrongs of the past has meant that even though legal discrimination has been mostly outlawed, socioeconomically, we are still living in the 1960s.

During the Civil Rights Movement, President Lyndon Johnson established the Kerner Commission to analyze the conditions that were resulting in ongoing, deadly race riots across the country. In the Commission's final report, they called on national and local leaders to make "massive and sustained" investments in jobs and education.[14] These investments were intended to reverse the "segregation and poverty [that] have created in the racial ghetto, a destructive environment totally unknown to most white Americans."[15]

Fifty years later, the Commission's lone surviving member concluded that "in many ways, things have gotten no better—or have gotten worse."[16]

The Map

Tying together these different manifestations of systemic racism, we get the following map.

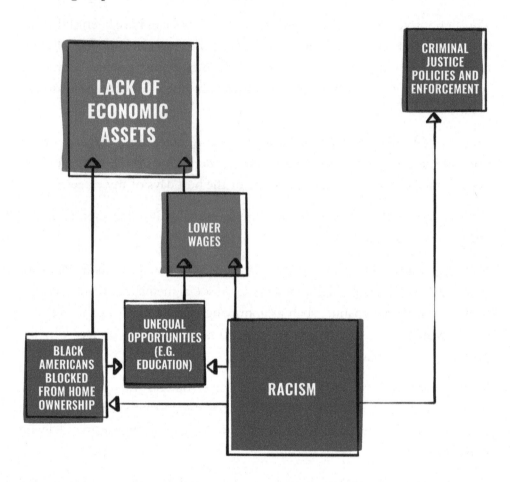

Chapter 10:
Mental Illness

This book opened with a paradox.

For the majority of people who experience it, homelessness is a relatively brief occurrence that is often resolved in a few short weeks or months.

To that end, over the last three chapters, we looked at the ways in which changing socioeconomic circumstances (the cost of housing, declining wages, limited access to savings and wealth) have made it more likely for a "shock" (an eviction, a rent increase, a job loss, a relational or health crisis) to push a household into homelessness as they grapple with short- to medium-term financial hardship.

That being said, when it comes to our most memorable encounters with the issue of homelessness, we often recall people who seem to have been homeless for years, even decades. While economic conditions are certainly a factor, these folks usually appear to have extreme social, emotional, and/or psychiatric challenges.

As just one example, I recently encountered a man who appeared to be panhandling in downtown Berkeley, CA. His sign read "please help" but he wasn't really asking for money. He sat cross-legged on the sidewalk, gyrating wildly from side-to-side. His hair was unkempt and his clothes were ragged. His mouth and jaw were hinging and grinding uncontrollably. His words and grunts were mostly indiscernible, and he seemed to be staring at something that wasn't actually there.

A few yards after passing him, I stopped and looked back. From a distance, I could see an invisible barrier around him. As people rushed by on the busy sidewalk, no one would get closer than ten feet. There was no eye contact. No one stopped or asked if he was ok.

Seeing this man suffer made me feel angry, sad, and powerless. Tears started pooling in my eyes. But just like everyone else, I turned around and kept walking.

Chronic Homelessness

I am willing to bet that when you think about homelessness, you recall situations like this. Over the past few years in the Bay Area, I can vividly remember:

- Being randomly screamed at by a clearly mentally ill woman while sitting outside at a café

- Witnessing people shooting up or passing out on corners or busy sidewalks, too intoxicated to function

- Seeing people so gravely disabled that they were covered in their own feces or living buried under mounds of trash, debris, and even active rodent infestations

While utterly heartbreaking, these scenes can also elicit understandable outrage – from small business owners, parents, and other community members. Even in progressive San Francisco, frustration over homelessness has ranged from creating apps that map incidents of human poop to Facebook rants lamenting that "The degenerates gather like hyenas, spit, urinate, taunt you … there is nothing positive gained from having [homeless people] so close to us. It's a burden and a liability."[1]

However you feel about this behavior, I would ask that you briefly suspend your judgment. Instead, take a moment to think about what would cause *you* to behave this way.

Seriously.

What sort of physical and/or emotional state would you have to be in to defecate on a busy sidewalk, to scream at people on the street, to refuse to wash for weeks or months at a time, or to eat garbage out of a public trash can?

However upset we might get about the antisocial impacts of homelessness, nine times out of 10, the light bulb immediately goes off when I walk people through this thought experiment. Healthy and psychologically well people do not engage in this type of behavior.

The Department of Housing & Urban Development defines chronic homelessness as long-term homelessness that is accompanied by a disability.[2] While the numbers can vary from community to community, approximately 10-30% of the overall homeless community is experiencing long-term, chronic homelessness.

NUMBER OF DISABLING CONDITIONS

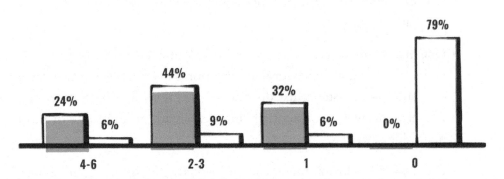

TYPE OF DISABLING CONDITIONS

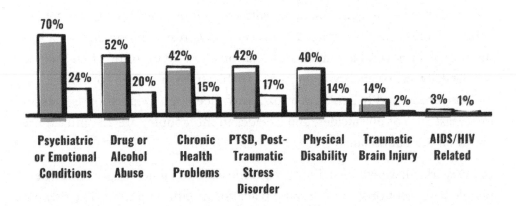

Looking at data from Marin County, we get a better sense of what "disabling conditions" are. For example, a staggering 65% of people experiencing chronic homelessness in Marin report having some type of psychiatric or emotional challenge.[3] Other examples might include a substance abuse disorder, Post-Traumatic Stress Disorder, a traumatic brain injury, a physical disability, a chronic health issue, or a developmental disability.

Among people experiencing chronic homelessness in Marin, 68% have more than two disabilities and 24% have more than four.[4]

Brain Disease / Impairment

According to the National Alliance on Mental Illness (NAMI):

- One in five Americans experience a mental health issue every year, such as an anxiety disorder or depression.[5]

- One in 25 Americans experience Serious Mental Illness (SMI) every year, which is a "mental, behavioral, or emotional disorder (excluding developmental and substance use disorders) ... resulting in serious functional impairment, which substantially interferes with or limits one or more major life activities."[6]

- One-half of all chronic mental illness begins by the age of 14; three-quarters by the age of 24.[7]

When it comes to SMI, which is particularly prevalent among people experiencing chronic homelessness, it is most common to see clinical depression, bipolar disorder, or schizophrenia.

A manual used to diagnose mental health conditions called the DSM-5 defines clinical depression as prolonged periods of a depressed mood and/or a loss of interest in normal activities and relationships.[8] Symptoms often include almost daily loss of energy, feelings of worthlessness, impaired concentration, indecisiveness, and hypersomnia (excessive sleeping). Depression is present in at least 50% of all suicides, and suicides in this country are 2.5 times more common than homicides.[9]

In my work, I have witnessed some extreme cases of clinical depression where people have slept or sat in the same place for months at a time. They would barely eat, end up soiling themselves, and could barely hold a conversation. In one case, a man said he was woken up at night by rats gnawing at the trash that had accumulated around his body.

Bipolar disorder is characterized by extended periods of depression and also extended periods of "mania," the opposite of depression. Mania can range from being elated and energized to full blown delusions. These delusions can include the belief that one can achieve superhuman feats or that one has transformed into a famous or powerful person.

This distorted thinking can lead to outlandish, violent, or generally inappropriate behavior. People can completely destroy their lives while in a manic state, like spending all of their savings on erratic purchases or abandoning family to engage in risky behavior.

It can be quite unsettling to witness someone experiencing a full-blown manic episode. In my work, I witnessed one person completely disrupt a downtown business corridor by routinely walking into businesses and screaming at customers. At other times, this person would set up lawn chairs or use golf clubs in the middle of downtown sidewalks.

Finally, schizophrenia is a long-term breakdown in the relationship between thought, emotion, and behavior. The breakdown can lead to faulty perception, hallucinations, paranoia, and delusions of grandeur.

Research has shown there are really two types of schizophrenia. One type of schizophrenic hears voices and has paranoid and disorganized thoughts, but they retain their basic personality. Their brain structure isn't that different (suggesting a possible chemical imbalance), and they do well on medications.

By comparison, the second type of schizophrenic has hardcore, psychotic symptoms. These individuals might be found wearing multiple layers of ragged clothing on a hot day or making outlandish claims like being the second coming of Jesus Christ or being stalked by the CIA. For these people, brain scans reveal significant structural damage to the brain, similar to what happens with dementia.

While Traumatic Brain Injury (TBI) is an altogether different challenge and disability (affecting cognitive, emotional, and physical wellbeing), it's worth noting that studies have found that upwards of 53% of people experiencing homelessness have TBI.[10]

Think about that for a moment. Up to half of all people experiencing home-lessness have severe and lasting damage inflicted on the most important organ in their body – their brain.

In this country, there is a tendency to moralize mental health. We think the uncomfortable behaviors stemming from a psychiatric illness are somehow a choice. But mental health conditions are more properly understood as forms of brain disease, similar to heart disease, kidney disease, cancer, or diabetes.

Deinstitutionalization

Despite what we know now about mental illness, for thousands of years it was profoundly misunderstood.

Often thought to be witchcraft, demonic possession, or simply moral short-comings, these misdiagnoses justified a variety of inhumane practices.

- In 30 AD, the Roman doctor Celsus argued that philosophy and personal strength were the key to recovery. To that end, he advocated treatments ranging from the wearing of amulets to physical torture.

- In 1483, the Pope sanctioned *Malleus Maleficarum,* or "Witches Hammer." This blamed the mentally ill for the Bubonic Plague and justified burning them at the stake. "Trephining" was also common in the middle ages. It was the practice of drilling a hole in someone's head so evil spirits could leave.

- In the 1700s, doctors often thought physical and mental health were connected. Thus, in an effort to manipulate the body in order to manip-ulate the mind, mentally ill patients were submerged in ice water baths, placed in physical restraints, and locked away in isolation.

The situation in the US was no different.

In the mid-1880s, towns contracted with local individuals to care for mentally ill people who could not care for themselves. Unregulated and underfunded, this system resulted in widespread abuse, and many vulnerable people ended up on the street or in jail.

In a report to the Massachusetts State Legislature, famed mental health reformer Dorothea Dix proclaimed: "I proceed, Gentlemen, briefly to call your attention to the present state of Insane Persons confined within this Commonwealth, in cages, stalls, pens! Chained, naked, beaten with rods, and lashed into obedience."[11]

Thanks to her efforts and others like her, the mental health system began to change. State-run hospitals emerged as a more humane place for people to go. While the word "asylum" has certain negative connotations today, at the time, asylums were seen as havens of safety and care.

In a way, however, the state hospital system was too successful. For the next 80 years, people with severe mental illness were no longer on America's streets, and the public gradually forgot that this had even been such a significant issue.

Sadly though, any system that skirts public accountability for almost a century is bound to develop problems.

In 1955, with over half a million Americans living in these facilities, Congress and President Eisenhower passed the Mental Health Study Act, which created a joint commission to investigate. Greer Williams, a prominent psychiatrist and writer, was the editor of the commission's final report. In a 1961 interview with *The Atlantic*, he reported that:

> Comparatively few of the 277 state hospitals — probably no more than 20% — have actively participated in the modern therapeutic trend toward humane, healing hospitals and clinics of easy access and easy exit, instead of locked, barred, prison-like depositories of alienated and rejected human beings ... [the typical state hospital] does a good job of keeping patients physically alive and mentally sick.[12]

Public support for state hospitals continued to erode, hastened by books like *One Flew Over the Cuckoo's Nest* (1962), with its graphic depictions of electroconvulsive therapy and unsympathetic portrayals of mental health workers.

At the same time, the 1950s and '60s also witnessed progress. New antipsychotic medications emerged, such as Thorazine. Although its effects varied from person to person, for the first time many people with severe and persistent mental illness could be reliably treated beyond the hospital walls.

As a result of these developments, a new vision for mental health treatment was beginning to emerge when John F. Kennedy became president in 1961. As JFK himself would go on to say, "We must move from the outmoded use of distant custodial institutions to the concept of community-centered agencies."[13]

To replace asylums, JFK envisioned a national network of community-based mental health centers equipped to provide "a coordinated range of timely diagnostic, health, educational, training, rehabilitation, employment, welfare, and legal protection services."[14] The "Community Mental Health Centers Act" (CMHCA) ended up being the last piece of legislation JFK signed into law before he was assassinated in 1963.

The shift to community-based treatment is generally referred to as deinstitutionalization.

If you were to measure the success of deinstitutionalization by the clearing out of state hospitals, it was a resounding success. Between 1955 and 1998, the populations in state and county mental health hospitals dropped from approximately 558,000 to fewer than 60,000.[15] Based on these numbers, today the US only has 6% of the per capita mental health bed capacity that it had in 1955.

This might suggest community-based mental health treatment is alive and well, but that's not what actually happened.

The 1960s witnessed massive investment in publicly-funded healthcare through programs like Medicaid and Medicare. By comparison, the Community Mental Health Act of 1963 was almost immediately gutted of its major funding provisions. In particular, nothing was set aside for staffing, even though the entire community-based treatment model was premised on staffing.

Funding has remained insufficient ever since.

In the last year of his presidency, Jimmy Carter signed the Mental Health Services Act (MHSA) of 1980, which provided more grant funding directly to community mental health centers. President Ronald Reagan went on to repeal most of MHSA in 1981 even after John Hinkley, Jr. – a man suffering from an untreated psychotic disorder – attempted to assassinate him in March of that same year.

There were glimmers of hope in the 1990s and 2000s. President George H. W. Bush passed the Americans with Disabilities Act. Presidents Bill Clinton and

George W. Bush required more mental health coverage from insurance providers.

Unfortunately, the Great Recession reversed much of this progress. Between 2009 and 2013, America's 50 state legislatures cut a total of $4.6 billion in services for the mentally ill, even as patient intakes were increasing.[16]

This downward trend continued under President Donald Trump. Following the 2017 murders of 17 young people at Marjory Stoneman Douglas High School in Florida, President Trump remarked that there were "so many signs that the Florida shooter was mentally disturbed, even expelled from school for bad and erratic behavior ... and classmates knew he was a big problem."[17] Regardless, the President later called for cutting the $668 million in funding for the Substance Abuse and Mental Health Services Administration.[18]

It's more, however, than just a lack of services and resources.

Mental Illness and the Courts

In the 1950s, it was clear that requiring involuntary medical treatment (known as the commitment process) had also been wildly abused. Family members were colluding with doctors to lock away spouses and elderly relatives, and patients were often subjected to treatment against their will.

To combat this abuse, in 1969, California passed the "Lanterman-Petris-Short" Act. In a few short years, the "LPS Commitment Process" had become the model for almost every state in the country.

The LPS Act created strict new standards for involuntary holds. The process essentially moved oversight away from healthcare providers and over to the criminal justice system.

It might sound odd to describe an expansion of civil liberties as a bad thing. In the context of serious mental illness, however, these reforms have in some cases resulted in the sickest people being unable to receive the treatment they desperately need precisely because they are so symptomatic.

In 1975 in *Donaldson vs. O'Connor*, not only did the US Supreme Court uphold the LPS concept, it went a step further, ruling that no one can be hospitalized involuntarily if that person can simply *"survive"* in the community. In some communities, eating trash out of dumpsters constitutes surviving.

In 1979 in *Reise v. St. Mary's*, the California Supreme Court gave mentally ill people the right to refuse treatment. The court also ruled that past behavior patterns may not be weighed as evidence. Instead, involuntary holds must be based on an "imminent" danger in the present moment.

In *Street Crazy: America's Mental Health Tragedy*, which informed much of the history in this chapter, Dr. Steven Seager writes about his work in a psychiatric emergency unit in Los Angeles. During this time he witnessed many extreme and graphic examples of the dysfunction made possible by our current laws and legal precedents.

> No one knew anything was wrong until [Pamela] took after her mother with a knife, stabbing the woman forty-seven times. That's when she mentioned the voices ... She was declared innocent by reason of insanity and committed ... for what everyone assumed would be a long time. Within a year, Pamela had been released. She'd cleared up on anti-psychotic medication and was once again considered fit for the community ... [but] back on the streets, she'd stop taking her medicine, the voices would return.[19]

As Dr. Seager recounts, this became a lifelong pattern for Pamela. Rather than attacking others again, she began mutilating herself during her psychotic episodes, such as cutting off the tips of her fingers and toes. She would be hospitalized, would improve on medication, and then she would be released within a few weeks, only to discontinue the treatment that had stabilized her.

On Pamela's *forty-ninth* visit to Dr. Seager's psych emergency unit, she had ripped off her eyelid below the brow.[20]

As stories like Pamela's sadly illustrate, by the early 1980s, it was apparent that something had gone terribly wrong.

"The policy that led to the release of most of the nation's mentally ill patients from the hospital to the community is now widely regarded as a major failure," declared *The New York Times* in 1984.[21]

"States proved more enthusiastic about emptying the old facilities than about providing new ones," the *Chicago Tribune* noted in 1989.[22] "Many patients went from straitjackets to steam grates."[23]

Frank Lanterman himself, co-author of the LPS Act, regretted how the law had evolved. "I wanted the law to help the mentally ill," he said. "I never meant for it to prevent those who need care from receiving it. The law has to be changed."[24]

In a sad sign of how far our mental health system has fallen, we have now boomeranged back to the ante-bellum paradigm that motivated Dorothea Dix 170 years ago.

- Rather than the hospitals those early activists advocated for, the three largest "institutional settings" for people with mental illness are now jails: Rikers Island, Cook County and Los Angeles County.[25]

- The National Alliance on Mental Illness estimates that approximately 40% of incarcerated Americans have a history of mental health issues, which is double the prevalence of mental illness in the general population.[26]

In addition to the challenges of navigating mental illness itself, we've already seen the way in which criminal justice interactions create barriers to employment. Unsurprisingly, the rate of unemployment among people receiving public mental health services is approximately 80%.[27]

The Map

Mental illness is a "behavioral health" issue, which is the more all-encompassing term for social and emotional wellbeing. Before adding behavioral health to our systems map, we need to look at the other major way it manifests in people experiencing homelessness – addiction.

Chapter 11: Addiction

Of all the upstream causes of homelessness, this is the one I can relate to the most.

I grew up with an alcoholic parent who, to this day, has been unable to stop drinking. As a result, I know firsthand the wreckage that addiction can bring to a family.

At the same time, despite my very best efforts to not go down the same path, I am also an alcoholic. Fortunately, after roughly 13 years, I was able to get on a path to recovery, which I remain on to this day.

Brain Disease – Part 2

In the last chapter we looked at how mental illness is a "brain disease."

Though we tend to moralize addiction even more than mental illness, it is the same dynamic. Addiction physically changes the biological structure and wiring of the brain. According to the National Institutes for Health:

> A healthy brain rewards healthy behaviors — like exercising, eating, or bonding with loved ones. It does this by switching on brain circuits that make you feel wonderful, which then motivates you to repeat those behaviors. In contrast, when you're in danger, a healthy brain pushes your body to react quickly with

fear or alarm, so you'll get out of harm's way. If you're tempted by something questionable — like eating ice cream before dinner or buying things you can't afford — the front regions of your brain can help you decide if the consequences are worth the actions.

But when you're becoming addicted to a substance, that normal hardwiring of helpful brain processes can begin to work against you. Drugs or alcohol can hijack the pleasure / reward circuits in your brain and hook you into wanting more and more. Addiction can also send your emotional danger-sensing circuits into overdrive, making you feel anxious and stressed when you're not using the drugs or alcohol. At this stage, people often use drugs or alcohol to keep from feeling bad rather than for their pleasurable effects.

To add to that, repeated use of drugs can damage the essential decision-making center at the front of the brain. This area, known as the prefrontal cortex, is the very region that should help you recognize the harms of using addictive substances.[1]

There is a genetic component to this.

Studies that look at the behavior of identical twins suggest that roughly 40-70% of substance abuse disorders can be accounted for by our genes.[2]

Simply put, we each come wired with different pleasure-recognition circuitry. This helps to account for why two people might consume similar amounts of drugs and alcohol, yet one person becomes an addict and the other doesn't.

This biological component is clearly very powerful, but from my own experience, as well as listening to the stories from countless others, in many cases there is more to addiction than simply biological predisposition.

Pain

In his outstanding book *In the Realm of Hungry Ghosts: Close Encounters with Addiction*, Dr. Gabor Mate draws on his experience working with heavily addicted patients in Vancouver's Downtown Eastside to formulate the following definition of addiction:

- Seeking out something that causes pleasure in the short-term

- Having that pleasure-seeking behavior cause problems in the long-term

- Despite the consequences, being unable to stop[3]

There are two critical insights from this definition.

First, we become addicted to "something." There is nothing about this cycle that is inherently limited to drugs and alcohol. There are plenty of pleasure-seeking activities that people can become addicted to: gambling, eating, working, shopping, watching pornography. According to Dr. Mate:

> Addiction is a continuum that extends from the disheveled street person using injectable drugs - whom we might avoid on street corners - to the well-dressed, successful workaholic, like a physician, who is addicted to recognition, fame, and self-promotion.[4]

Second, as we saw with the overview of addiction from the National Institutes for Health, there is nothing inherently wrong with seeking pleasure. The problem of addiction arises when pleasure-seeking behavior becomes a strategy for dealing with some other underlying problem.

According to Dr. Mate, it is impossible to understand addiction without asking what relief the addict finds, or hopes to find, in the drug or the addictive behavior. Put differently, the question is not why the addiction, it's why the pain?[5]

One way to think about this perspective is to consider the traditional, substance-driven explanation of addiction, which hypothesizes that all or most people who use a substance beyond a certain minimum amount become addicted.

This theory grew out of studies beginning in the 1960s, when addiction researchers began creating experiments that allowed animals to self-administer drugs. As animals in these clinical settings began consuming these substances as much as they possibly could, it seemed to suggest that there was an inherent addictive quality to mind-altering chemicals.[6]

Other researchers, however, began to question some of the underlying assumptions in these experiments.

For example, in the 1970s, Canadian psychologist Bruce K. Alexander pioneered a new approach to this classic experiment. Alexander theorized that instead of the substances, opiate dependence was attributable to environmental conditions.[7] Specifically, the animals in these studies had been forced to live in sterile, confined cages, often in some form of isolation. Could that have had an impact on substance use?

To test his theory, Alexander built "Rat Park," a housing colony approximately 200 times more spacious than a regular laboratory cage. Half a dozen rats of both sexes lived together with ample provision of food, toys, and space for socializing, mating, and raising litters.

Unlike the original experiments, the Rat Park rats had little appetite for morphine.

In fact, rats that had been forced to consume opiates daily for nearly two months were brought to Rat Park and given the opportunity to choose between tap or opiate-laced water. Alexander found that even the most "addicted" rats chose plain water.

Of course, rats are one thing, but what about people?

It's extremely difficult (and morally problematic) to run controlled experiments like Rat Park on human beings; however, there are occasions and environments where people are put under significant stress and pain, such as war.

During the Vietnam War, many American soldiers became addicted to heroin. Amazingly though, despite our cultural fear about the potency of drugs like heroin, only 5% of previously addicted soldiers still met the criteria for addiction just ten months after returning home.[8]

A 95% recovery rate is absolutely unheard of and cannot simply be accounted for by treatment only.

There are other even more recent examples of pervasive, community-wide pain.

Over the last 20 years, our country has witnessed steady increases in rates of suicides and drug overdoses, with the latter increasing by 500% since 1990.[9] In 2020 alone, over 100,000 people died of overdoses.[10]

Interestingly, the underlying cause of these increases can, in part, be traced back to Chapter 7 and our exploration of the labor participation rate.

The current epidemic of suicides and overdoses is not happening uniformly across the country. A 2017 study found that as the unemployment rate increases by one percentage point in a given county, the opioid-death-rate rises by 3.6%, and emergency-room visits rise by 7%.[11]

In other words, the pain of economic dislocation and financial instability can drive many to overuse drugs and alcohol, or even take their own lives.

Adverse Childhood Experiences (ACEs)

When it comes to pain fueling addiction, however, one source seems to trump all else. I have observed this in the recovery community and also among people experiencing homelessness. I can even attest to it on a personal level. Sometimes the most painful wounds are the earliest.

In the wonderful book *The Deepest Well: Healing the Long-Term Effects of Childhood Adversity*, the State of California's Surgeon General Nadine Burke Harris recounts a powerful discovery of the lasting link between early childhood experiences and later health issues.

In the 1980s, the Kaiser Permanente hospital system opened an obesity clinic in San Diego, CA. The center developed a highly effective framework using a rigorous diet and exercise program to help people lose weight. The program was full of dramatic success stories, but 50% of participants dropped out of the program, even after they had lost weight.

To figure out how to improve retention, Dr. Vincent Felitti was tasked with interviewing dropouts. One interview subject was named Patty.

In 1985, Patty was 28 years old and weighed 405 pounds. With the help of the program, she lost 276 pounds in less than a year.

Patty maintained this weight loss for a period of time, but then she suddenly reversed course, gaining 37 pounds in just one month.

Felitti suspected something must have triggered this dramatic change, and his hunch proved correct. Patty went on to describe how there was a new client at work who was much older and married. After she lost weight, he complimented and sexually propositioned her. Felitti countered that, though the sexual advances were understandably inappropriate and unpleasant, extreme weight gain seemed like a strange response. That's when Patty revealed that her grandfather began raping her when she was 10. The start of her over-eating coincided with the start of this sexual abuse.

Shockingly, as Felitti talked to more former program participants, he discovered that a majority of the 286 people he interviewed had experienced childhood sexual abuse. This suggested that for many, weight gain somehow correlated with this extremely traumatic childhood experience.

To validate these initial findings, Felitti joined forces with Robert Anda from the Centers for Disease Control and Prevention. They surveyed 17,337 Kaiser Permanente patient volunteers to investigate the long-term consequences of childhood trauma and abuse on health outcomes.

In what became known as the Adverse Childhood Experience (ACE) study, participants were asked about 10 different types of childhood trauma that had been identified in earlier research literature.[12] This included:

- Abuse (physical, verbal, sexual)

- Neglect (physical emotional)

- Household dysfunction (mental illness, substance abuse, incarcerated relative, domestic violence, divorce)

PREVALENCE OF INDIVIDUAL ACEs

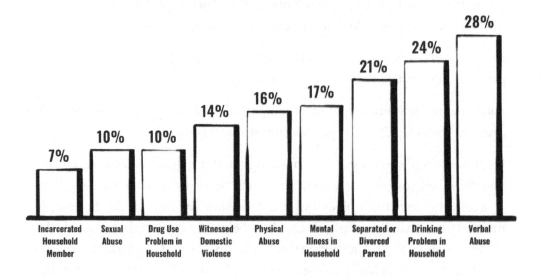

94

Countless follow-up studies have all corroborated similar findings from the original ACE research initiative:

- Abuse, neglect, and household dysfunction in childhood can have a lifelong impact on a person's health.[13]

- Roughly 60% of Americans have at least one point on the 10-point scale, and up to 17% have four or more points.[14]

- There is a "dose-response" relationship between ACE scores and health outcomes.[15] This means, the more trauma, the worse the health outcomes.

This final point is extremely important because the same dose dependent phenomenon appears with substance use disorders too. Compared to a person with zero ACEs, a person with four or more ACEs is:[16]

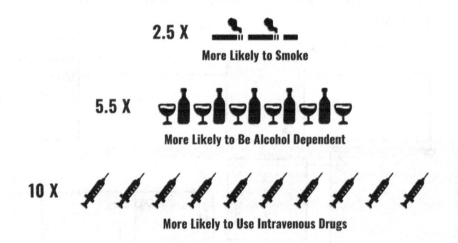

2.5 X
More Likely to Smoke

5.5 X
More Likely to Be Alcohol Dependent

10 X
More Likely to Use Intravenous Drugs

For intravenous drug use specifically, people who have endured *six or more ACEs are 4,600%* more likely to inject drugs than someone with zero ACEs.[17]

As Dr. Mate powerfully puts it:

> We can be moved by the tragedy of mass starvation on a far continent. Afterall, we have all known physical hunger, if only temporarily. But it takes a greater effort of emotional imagination to empathize with the addict. We readily feel for a suffering child but cannot see the child in the adult, who - whose soul fragmented and isolated – hustles for survival a few blocks away from where we shop and work.[18]

The Map

As I began learning more about the underlying causes of addiction and how they would impact our systems map, I started seeing my own story in these elements and interconnections.

Having an alcoholic parent predisposed me to also developing a substance use disorder. That predisposition alone might have been enough to tilt me toward alcoholism, but trauma and abuse within the household made it even likelier.

This story, and the millions like it, speak to the powerful "generational nature" of a problem like addiction. If there is active addiction in a family, not only are future generations at greater genetic risk, but addictive behavior from family members can generate enough pain and trauma that it triggers the predisposition.

This is a vicious feedback loop perpetuating addiction from grandparents to parents to children.

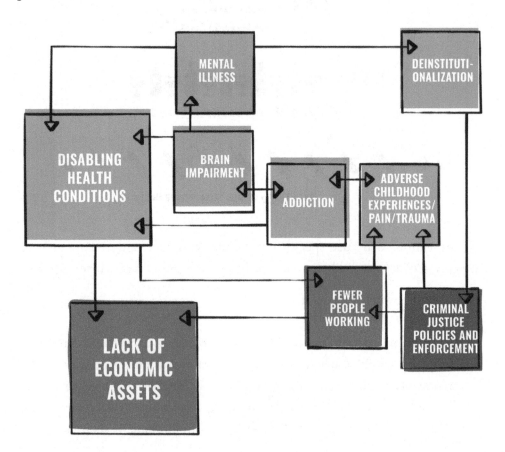

Chapter 12:
The Modern Homelessness Crisis

Homelessness is a very old problem in this country, yet it has manifested in different ways for different reasons throughout our history.

Chapters 7, 8, 9, 10, and 11 looked at some of the most significant contributing factors to what I call "The Modern Homelessness Crisis." So, what have we learned?

Seeing the System

Tying together the insights from the last few chapters, we get the following picture of The Modern Homelessness Crisis.

Importantly, I see this systems map as a living artifact that can and should change over time. If you are interested in sharing your thoughts and perspective, I would encourage you to visit:

www.howtosolvehomelessness.org.

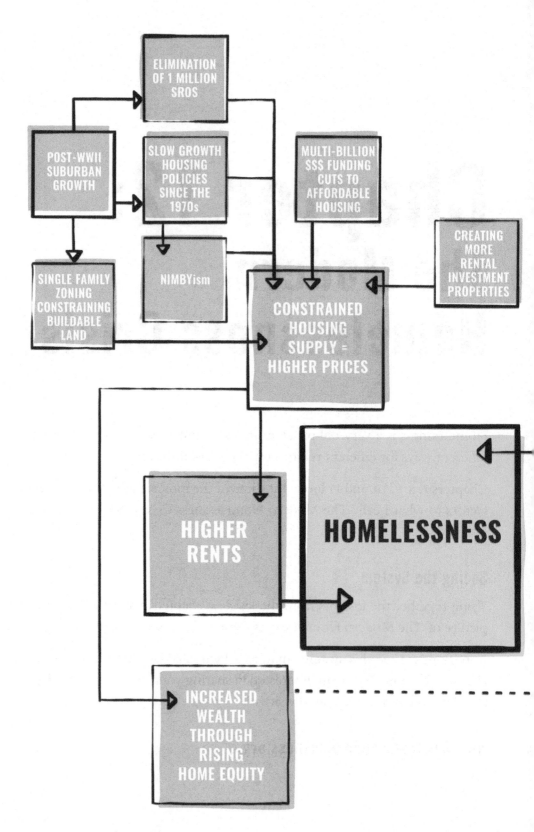

ELIMINATION OF 1 MILLION SROS

POST-WWII SUBURBAN GROWTH

SLOW GROWTH HOUSING POLICIES SINCE THE 1970s

MULTI-BILLION $$$ FUNDING CUTS TO AFFORDABLE HOUSING

CREATING MORE RENTAL INVESTMENT PROPERTIES

SINGLE FAMILY ZONING CONSTRAINING BUILDABLE LAND

NIMBYism

CONSTRAINED HOUSING SUPPLY = HIGHER PRICES

HIGHER RENTS

HOMELESSNESS

INCREASED WEALTH THROUGH RISING HOME EQUITY

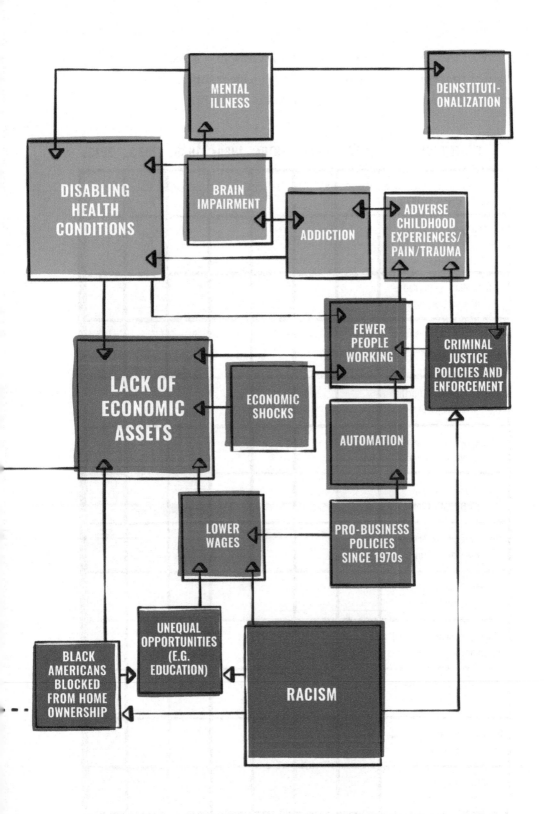

In terms of the timing of The Modern Homelessness Crisis, when we chart the history of these different subsystems, we see a clear shift in the socioeconomic fabric of our country during the 1970s and early 1980s.

SYSTEM ISSUE	1950s	1960s	1970s	1980s	1990s	2000s	2010s
Increased housing regulation and the rise of NIMBYism		▓	▓	▓	▓	▓	▓
The lasting impact of eliminating 1 million SRO units		▓	▓	▓	▓	▓	▓
Defunding of affordable housing programs				▓	▓	▓	▓
Rise in investment properties and online platforms						▓	▓
Wage stagnation for the average worker			▓	▓	▓	▓	▓
Rising rates of income and wealth inequality			▓	▓	▓	▓	▓
A declining labor participation rate					▓	▓	▓
The increased prosecution of the War on Drugs			▓	▓	▓	▓	▓
Increasing rates of incarceration				▓	▓	▓	▓
Deinstitutionalization and the untreated mental illness		▓	▓	▓	▓	▓	▓
Defunding of mental health services and programs				▓	▓	▓	▓
Ongoing impacts of systemic racism	▓	▓	▓	▓	▓	▓	▓
Societal and personal pain fueling addiction	▓	▓	▓	▓	▓	▓	▓

While there are many issues at play, this analysis points to one fundamental dynamic: rent keeps going up, and for a wide variety of reasons – racism, pro-business economic policies, mental illness, addiction – people do not have the economic assets to cover that cost.

To put hard numbers to this, according to a study from Harvard University, between 1960 to 2016, adjusting for inflation, the median American rent payment rose 61% while the median renter's income increased by only 5%.[1]

INSIGHT #5	Rent keeps going up, and for a wide variety of reasons – racism, pro-business economic policies, mental illness, addiction – people have fewer economic assets to cover that cost.

Shocks vs. Structure

Importantly, by using systems thinking to observe the broader historical context of the past 40 years, we can more easily see how recent "shocks" like the Great Recession and the COVID-19 Pandemic, which have each certainly made homelessness worse in their own right, are more accurately understood as exacerbations of deeper, more underlying problems, such as economic inequality.

As systems theorist Daniel Kim describes in his "Iceberg" framework,

> *Events* are the occurrences we encounter on a day-to-day basis ... *Patterns* are the accumulated "memories" of events. When strung together as a series over time, they can reveal recurring trends ... *Systemic structures* are the ways in which the parts of a system are organized. These structures actually generate the patterns and events we observe.[2]

The Modern Homelessness Crisis is not an independent problem resulting from the collective decision of millions of people to suddenly be homeless.

No, the homelessness that we observe today is a symptom of profound structural problems. It is the inevitable result of increasingly untenable societal choices that impact the options available to the most vulnerable among us.

Part 3:
A Failed Response

Chapter 13:
A Predictable Reaction

Imagine it's the early 1980s. You're an elected leader in your city, town, or county, and you start to see a wave of new people living on the streets in your community.

While you might be able to connect the dots among some of the issues we've looked at so far, many of these changes are happening outside of the control of any individual local jurisdiction. Regardless, community members are upset and demanding immediate action.

What would you do?

In 2015, Bay Area media outlets teamed up to launch the "SF Homeless Project," a now multi-year effort to better explain homelessness in the region. In one particularly excellent article, reporters attempted to tackle this very question by exploring the shifting strategies of five different San Francisco Mayors as told through their own public statements.[1]

By the time I read this article, I had worked in six different jurisdictions in the Bay Area (not including San Francisco). Thus, I was surprised to find myself nodding along as I read the various approaches each mayor took.

My agreement stemmed from having seen each of these strategies before. That's when it dawned on me – there is a predictable progression to how communities respond to homelessness. In fact, these responses map to well-trodden psychological literature.

The Five Stages of Grief

Inspired by her work with terminally ill patients, Swiss-American psychiatrist Elisabeth Kubler-Ross developed the "five stages of grief" model in the 1960s.[2] This framework was based on the observation that there is a predictable series of emotional states experienced by terminally ill patients after a diagnosis:

- Denial

- Anger

- Depression

- Bargaining

- Acceptance

As Kübler-Ross refined her model throughout her career, she added two important caveats:

1. These emotional responses applied more broadly than just terminal illnesses. They can chart our reaction to any difficult or new situation.[3]

2. The stages are not linear and predictable. Individuals can bounce between these stages, with some people never progressing to the final levels of bargaining and acceptance.[4]

Just as an individual might receive unexpected and unpleasant medical news, communities can similarly be hit with unexpected and unpleasant social developments, such as homelessness. And just like an individual person, these events can create community-wide denial, anger, and depression, but hopefully, also bargaining and acceptance.

As we'll see over the next few chapters, these different emotional responses tend to inform different strategic responses to homelessness. Let's start with the first three: denial, anger, and depression.

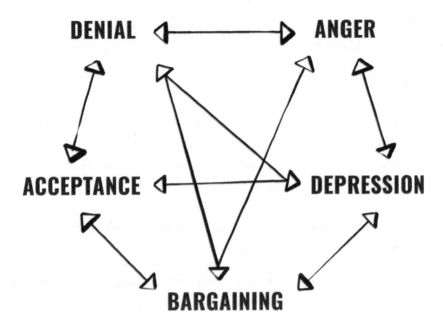

DENIAL ⟵⟶ ANGER

ACCEPTANCE ⟵ DEPRESSION

BARGAINING

Denial – The Natural Disaster Model

Art Agnos served as the Mayor of San Francisco from 1988 until 1992. Reflecting on the start of his term, Mayor Agnos recalled:

> When I became mayor in 1988, existing government policy for homelessness consisted of the "American disaster model" employed in natural disasters like floods and tornadoes. Cities opened armories and served coffee and doughnuts in what was expected to be temporary relief. Afterward, the homeless "victims" would resume their lives.[5]

In almost every community where I've worked, at some point in the 1980s (or even the 1970s) there was strong public support for the "disaster response" model. As Mayor Agnos observed, this typically looked like the creation of respite-type services such as soup kitchens, emergency shelters, or even service centers with mail, showers, and social workers.

However these programs originated, their goal was generally to meet the immediate, basic needs of people experiencing homelessness.

As we've learned, many people do in fact benefit from a light touch and quickly resolve their homelessness. At the same time, others continue to struggle, especially when they have more severe and persistent challenges, such as mental illness and/or addiction.

Mayor Agnos understood that:

> My administration recognized that the homelessness created by disasters like drug abuse, mental illness, domestic violence, alcoholism, runaway children, unemployment or low wages required a different approach than homelessness created by floods and hurricanes.[6]

So San Francisco began investing more significantly into intensive, wraparound services and professional support staff.

While this local investment was a great step, it was completely insufficient for addressing the scale and scope of the systemic issues we looked at in Part 2.

As San Francisco's leaders would come to learn, when an expensive response is mounted and fails to deliver, people get angry.

Anger – Criminalization

Frank Jordan served as Mayor of San Francisco from 1992 until 1996. Before being elected to office, Jordan was the city's police chief.

In response to growing frustration about homelessness, Jordan implemented the "Matrix Program," which was designed as a balance of love / tough love for the homeless community.

> Matrix was delivered through teams, each with a police officer, a public health worker and a social worker. The social worker would attempt to sign up homeless individuals for [services] ... The police officer would enforce laws against public inebriation, obstructing the sidewalks, trespassing, aggressive panhandling, public defecation or camping, and sleeping in neighborhood parks. We found we can't be tolerant of inappropriate behavior or it will only get worse.[7]

I have spent roughly half my career as a nonprofit service provider and the other half in local government.

The absolute hardest part of working within government (particularly a city) was striking a balance between supporting the humanity of people living on the street while also upholding basic public health and safety standards.

Take the example of encampments.

We tend to instinctively know an encampment when we observe one, but what exactly is "it" that we're seeing?

According to the federal Department of Housing and Urban Development, encampments have connotations of both impermanence and continuity.[8] They may be:

- A core group of people who are known to one another and who move together to different locations when necessary

- A changing group of people who cycle in and out of a single location

- An area comprised of tents or lean-to shacks built with scavenged materials

- People living in groups of cars, RVs, or other vehicles.[9]

In a state like California, encampments are the inevitable result of a lack of shelter. As of 2019, California was only able to provide night-to-night emergency shelter for approximately 30% of people experiencing homelessness.[10]

On one hand, how could we possibly punish people if they truly have nowhere else to go? Indeed, recent court rulings such as *Martin v. Boise* have found that it is unconstitutional to cite or arrest someone for sleeping outside if a community lacks alternative shelter accommodations.

On the other hand, the location of and behaviors within encampments can make them extremely difficult to tolerate.

For example, encampments can harbor human waste and rodent infestations. These have contributed to outbreaks of Hepatitis A and typhus among the homeless community.[11]

It is also my experience that people on the street are much more likely to be the victims of crime than the perpetrators, and as encampments grow, they can begin to harbor exploitative, criminal elements that lead to violent assault, sexual assault, robbery, and/or drug dealing.

Community safety is a totally understandable concern. But rather than solving the underlying causes that create encampments, frustrated and fearful communities often turn to the short-term tool of law enforcement.

Communities are never going to arrest their way out of this issue.

As we saw with the labor participation rate in Chapter 7, it becomes much harder to regain employment and housing when people have a criminal record. Thus, criminalizing homelessness becomes a vicious feedback loop that perpetuates the very problem it is trying to solve.

Many police officers wholeheartedly agree with the futility of this approach. In a 2018 op-ed entitled "Police Bear Increasingly Heavy Burden of Society's Problems," a former police chief in Marin County wrote:

> The role of peace officers has shifted dramatically in the last decade. It's never been more complex, challenging or dangerous for peace officers. All of society's most difficult problems have become daily concerns for the police. Homelessness, substance abuse and mental illness have become the primary daily activities of peace officers. Far too often the police are the wrong intervention for these societal issues, resulting in unintended outcomes, both for the officer and the person in crisis.[12]

Depression – Mitigation and Management

After failed attempts to balance a limited social service response with law enforcement, local leaders tend to reach the same defeated conclusion. As San Francisco Mayor Willie Brown (1996-2004) famously declared at the turn of the century, "Homelessness is unsolvable."[13]

This, I believe, is where most communities find themselves. After 40 years of failing to solve this crisis, homelessness does in fact feel unsolvable, and the only options left are attempting to mitigate issues like loitering, trash, and encampments while celebrating any limited success stories of jobs and housing.

When communities get to this point, they can become desperate for innovation.

After my year with AmeriCorps VISTA, I started working for a nonprofit that provided volunteer work experience opportunities for people experiencing homelessness. The goal was to help people regain the skills and experience they needed to find regular employment.

This model was marketed as a win-win-win for any community. For a couple hundred thousand dollars, a city or town would get a team of 20-30 current or formerly homeless individuals wearing highly visible, well-branded uniforms.

They provided the tangible benefit of cleaning up litter, removing graffiti, and clearing debris from homeless encampments. The community could feel good about investing in vulnerable people who wanted to "be part of the solution," and the team members had real opportunities to regain employment and housing, not to mention self-esteem and a sense of belonging.

Working with our team members was by far the highlight of my career. There has truly been nothing better than building one-on-one relationships with people and seeing their lives transform.

Despite this overwhelmingly positive experience, what I failed to fully appreciate at that time was the way in which our work fit into the broader "mitigation and management" strategy. To put it bluntly, how was a program for 20-30 people in a community with hundreds or even thousands of people experiencing homelessness ever going to solve anything?

Back then, in the face of those daunting numbers, I always thought the solution was simply to give our organization more funding. Afterall, with more resources, we could serve more people.

Maybe that was the solution. There was just one problem. What about all the other local service providers who felt exactly the same way about their programs?

Chapter 14:
The Homeless
Industrial Complex

One of the most powerful insights from systems thinking is that system components (goals, feedback loops, flows) tend to configure themselves in predictable ways. These regular patterns are called "system archetypes."

When you familiarize yourself with these archetypes, it becomes clear that many of society's biggest challenges are just different versions of the same underlying systemic patterns.

"The [INSERT INDUSTRY] Industrial Complex"

In 1961, President Dwight D. Eisenhower made the following observation during his farewell address from public office:

> Until the latest of our world conflicts, the United States had no armaments industry. American makers of plowshares could, with time and as required, make swords as well. But we can no longer risk emergency improvisation of national defense. We have been compelled to create a permanent armaments industry of vast proportions. Added to this, three and a half million men and women are directly engaged in the defense establishment. We annually spend on military

security alone more than the net income of all United States corporations.

Now this conjunction of an immense military establishment and a large arms industry is new in the American experience. The total influence—economic, political, even spiritual—is felt in every city, every Statehouse, every office of the Federal government. We recognize the imperative need for this development. Yet, we must not fail to comprehend its grave implications. Our toil, resources, and livelihood are all involved; so is the very structure of our society.

In the councils of government, we must guard against the acquisition of unwarranted influence, whether sought or unsought, by the military-industrial complex. The potential for the disastrous rise of misplaced power exists and will persist.

We must never let the weight of this combination endanger our liberties or democratic processes. We should take nothing for granted. Only an alert and knowledgeable citizenry can compel the proper meshing of the huge industrial and military machinery of defense with our peaceful methods and goals, so that security and liberty may prosper together.[1]

Over time, the term "[insert industry] industrial complex" has come to connote nefarious and self-serving tendencies within a given economic sector. It is:

A socioeconomic concept wherein businesses become entwined in social or political systems or institutions, creating or bolstering a profit economy from these systems. Such a complex is said to pursue its own financial interests regardless of, and often at the expense of, the best interests of society and individuals. Businesses within an industrial complex may have been created to advance a social or political goal, but mostly profit when the goal is not reached. The industrial complex may profit financially from maintaining socially detrimental or inefficient systems.[2]

To be very clear, in all of the time I have been working to end homelessness, collaborating with hundreds if not thousands of colleagues, I have not once met a person who is "pro-homelessness." There is no grand, corrupt conspiracy to perpetuate homelessness for the enrichment of those working in this space. Every person I have met in this field is genuine in their desire to help people and make a difference. And frankly, I think social workers and care providers should be more highly compensated, given the stress, demands, and importance of this work.

Nonetheless, on many occasions over the last decade, angry community members have alleged that my colleagues and I are in fact part of the "homeless industrial complex."

While this insinuation certainly stings, in all fairness, the social service sector as an "industry" is not above reproach. Here again we can turn to the wisdom of Donella Meadows:

> The destruction [these archetypes] cause is often blamed on particular actors or events, although it is actually a consequence of system structure. Blaming, disciplining, firing, twisting policy levers harder, hoping for a more favorable sequence of driving events, tinkering at the margins – these standard responses will not fix structural problems. That is why I call these archetypes "traps."[3]

No one wants homelessness, but over time, because society has failed to take the necessary steps to prevent it from happening in the first place, a large and robust homeless service system has emerged to try to help people regain housing.

Unfortunately, as anyone who has worked in this field will know all too well, structural inefficiencies often emerge as these social service systems grow, which makes solving homelessness even harder than it already is.

#1: Silos

"Silos" form when departments, organizations, or agencies operate independently without sharing information or coordinating activities. Silos exist in almost every industry, but they are particularly egregious when it comes to homelessness.

Part of the issue is the complexity of homelessness itself.

Do you remember David's story from Chapter 4? He suffered a traumatic brain injury in high school, which resulted in lifelong memory and aggression issues. Those challenges, in turn, contributed to nearly 40 years of homelessness.

There are Davids all across the country, and there is no single agency responsible for helping people like him. Instead, multiple organizations get involved with people like David, often with no knowledge or coordination around what's happening with other providers.

In Marin County, we started mapping out cases like David. The number of organizations involved was astounding:

- Multiple police departments

- Multiple nonprofit service providers

- County mental health

- The district attorney's office

- The public defender

- The public guardian

- The local psychiatric emergency unit

- Jail staff

- Jail mental health staff

- Local emergency medical services

- Local hospitals

Again, none of these individual organizations wanted David to be homeless. Everyone wanted him to get the help he needed. The problem was that the system was not inherently designed to facilitate the collaboration necessary to get him back inside.

When it comes to homelessness, we see silos at every level of government.

In California, the State itself does not have a unified plan or strategy for addressing homelessness that actually holds communities accountable. Instead, every city (there are 482) and county (there are 58) is more or less on its own to address homelessness as it sees fit.

Zooming in even further, in San Francisco, there are approximately 100 different nonprofit and governmental service providers operating over 200 different programs that in some capacity serve people experiencing homelessness.[4] It is nearly impossible to effectively coordinate all of these efforts.

#2: Poor Data and Anecdotal Successes

When communities are not coordinated and lack the ability to share data across partners, it's impossible to effectively measure what works and what does not.

The gold standard for measuring the effectiveness of any intervention is a double-blind study.

To conduct a double-blind study, researchers find a pool of people with similar characteristics (like age, physical abilities, interest in finding work). Then they randomly assign those people to different programs or even a control group (i.e., no program at all). With this type of methodology, neither the participants nor the experimenters know who is receiving a particular treatment, which helps to prevent bias.

After a certain period of time, researchers review the data and determine which interventions helped the most people. Ideally, this information would then help guide communities to do more of what works and less of what doesn't.

When it comes to homelessness, this level of evaluation rarely happens. Again, this isn't nefarious. I truly believe communities and organizations would if they could, but a big limitation is capacity. Very few communities have the resources (people, funding) to conduct rigorous studies like this.

As a consequence, when programs celebrate their successes, it is often self-reported from the organization itself. Self-reporting can make it extremely difficult to make apples-to-apples comparisons across programs, particularly if programs have different "enrollment requirements."

Imagine a program designed to get people jobs. The program might claim it is low barrier and open to all, but when you dig into the details, you learn that the program:

- Requires strict sobriety

- Participants must have a driver's license

- Participants cannot have a criminal record

We might nod along that these types of requirements make sense, but we have to acknowledge the bias they can create. If a program with all of these rules claims that "90% of training participants secure full-time employment," what would happen if we added back all of the people who were initially screened out and disqualified? Would the graduation rate really look more like 50%? That's not quite as impressive.

Importantly, this is where we can also see racial inequities emerge within the social service sector.

Sticking with this particular employment program, because Black Americans are disproportionately impacted by the criminal justice system, as we learned in Chapter 9, a program that disqualifies potential clients because of previous criminal justice involvement will inevitably disproportionately impact Black clients. While the program might not explicitly deny access to Black Americans, its requirements effectively do.

Because of this selection bias, it is particularly important to scrutinize one-off success stories. Yes, there are incredibly moving and heartwarming stories of people going from living on the street to earning $100,000 at a tech company. However, unless every client is experiencing outcomes like that, is the program really delivering what it's claiming?

#3: Credentialing

Despite the challenge of getting good data, it does exist. Yet even when there is strong evidence that a certain intervention works, there are rarely social service "credentialing" bodies to make sure communities or organizations are implementing the process correctly.

For example, "Housing First," which we'll learn more about in Part 4, is *an extremely effective intervention for solving long-term, chronic homelessness.* In a 2020 double-blind study from the University of California, San Francisco, one of the top medical research universities in the world, researchers found that "Housing First" keeps people housed 93% of the time.[5]

When it comes to interventions like "Housing First," I occasionally hear service providers say that they tried it, but it didn't work. In my experience, this is usually because the data-driven approach was not implemented.

If I buy a new sofa but don't follow the instructions to install all four legs, that sofa isn't going to work either. It's the same thing with social service interventions. Studies test a particular implementation process. If that process isn't followed, then the same results are unlikely to occur.

Compared to professional groups or regulatory bodies that uphold industry standards in sectors like healthcare (American Medical Association), criminal justice (BAR Associations), or construction (Occupational Health and Safety Administration), there is no credentialing body when it comes to homeless services.

As a consequence, there is no inherent accountability structure even when there is good data about what works.

#4: Boutique-ization

At the end of the last chapter, we saw how frustrated communities often reach a point where they are simply trying to mitigate the impacts of homelessness. When communities reach this point, I have repeatedly observed a strong desire and openness to "try something new."

Innovation is a great thing and it is very much needed. The problem is that rather than embarking on a systems-wide transformation or even looking at data driven solutions like "Housing First," many communities simply seek out programmatic novelty, such as funding pilot programs designed to serve a small number of people.

For example, when I first started working in San Rafael, CA, I was managing a brand-new program with a contractual goal of serving 12 people at any given time. In a community with 300+ people experiencing homelessness at any given time, this was never going to make a dent.

I have had countless conversations over the years with people who have an idea for the "next big thing" in homelessness. As I sit here finishing this chapter, I have an email in my inbox about a new Silicon Valley startup planning to "leverage artificial intelligence to revolutionize the homeless service system."

INSIGHT #6	Many communities end up with well-intentioned but uncoordinated homeless service systems whose structural inefficiencies can perpetuate the very problems they are intended to solve.

At best, "boutique" pilot programs are often well-intentioned efforts that end up only helping a limited number of people.

At worst, however, this type of scattershot innovation just adds to an already complex, unregulated, and siloed web of services, thus perpetuating the "homeless industrial complex" and making homelessness even harder to solve.

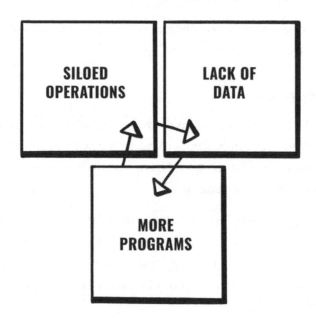

Chapter 15:
Rationalizing Inaction

I concluded the last chapter by critiquing certain aspects of the social service sector; however, any community that invests resources to address homelessness deserves recognition.

Indeed, this simple willingness to "do something" is one of the most important ingredients needed for ending The Modern Homelessness Crisis, yet for many communities, this first step is often the hardest.

San Rafael's Best Interest

In 2016, I started working in local government in San Rafael, a medium-sized city located in Marin County, CA.

A few years into that position, local housing advocates began demanding that the City and County create a permanent homeless shelter.

Over the previous 10 winters, the local faith-based community had organized a program called the Rotating Emergency Shelter Team (REST). Congregations took turns providing overnight shelter to 80 men and women during the coldest and wettest months of the year.

Thousands of local residents had volunteered with the program. It was beloved and, in many ways, had become an institution.

After a decade the organizers felt local government agencies needed to step up and create a permanent, year-round shelter that wasn't dependent on volunteers.

In a county with nearly 800 people experiencing unsheltered homelessness at that time, it seemed like a reasonable ask.

As the proposal began gaining momentum, San Rafael's Mayor asked me to lunch. He wanted to discuss the City's position, and that's when the strangest thing happened. Over the course of our meal, the Mayor started advocating in support of locating the countywide shelter in San Rafael. I – the City's Director of Homeless Planning and Outreach – began arguing against it.

My position had been created, in part, to address community frustration about the amount of homelessness in San Rafael.

Historically in Marin County, the vast majority of homeless services had been located in San Rafael, even though the Point-in-Time Count consistently found that 75% of Marin County's homeless community resided *outside* of San Rafael.[1] There was understandable resentment among San Rafael residents that other cities and towns in the county didn't appear to be contributing their fair share to the solution, and I was concerned that locating a permanent shelter in San Rafael would perpetuate those feelings.

Since starting in my role, I had been involved with numerous efforts to create more countywide services (outreach services, landlord recruitment efforts, housing developments), and I believed the same strategy should apply to shelter. Others needed to step up, too.

Though there might have been some logic to this, when I left that meeting, something wasn't sitting right. In advocating for the best interest of the jurisdiction where I worked, I was also arguing against my own moral compass – that every human being deserves the dignity of having a roof over their head and that I should seize every opportunity to make that a reality.

This dilemma of doing something in your own self-interest even if it hurts the greater good (even a greater good you support) is certainly not limited to homelessness.

We don't want trash, litter, or debris in our oceans, yet we continue to use single-use plastic products. We don't want to destroy our air quality and environment, yet we drive gas-powered cars.

Just like our exploration of "industrial complexes" in the last chapter, thanks to systems thinking, we now know that when we see patterns like this, there might be a system archetype at play.

Tragedy of the Commons

"Tragedy of the Commons" is one of the most well-known and well-researched system archetypes. It was first identified in the early 1800s in England.

Back at that time, England was still a rural, agricultural society, and most Britains depended on the land for their livelihood, either through farming or raising animals. Over hundreds of years, English villages had gradually developed a custom whereby herders could graze their cows on shared parcels of land called "commons."

The term "Tragedy of the Commons" originated in an essay written in 1833 by the British economist William Forster Lloyd.[2] He was interested in how herders shared this common land.

As with any scarce and finite resource, Lloyd reasoned that a given amount of land could only support a certain level of animal grazing. As a group, if the herders allowed too much grazing, the land would eventually be overused. Thus, the herders needed to coordinate in a way to ensure that overgrazing did not occur.

At the same time, each individual herder was economically incentivized to graze as much as possible. The more an individual grazed, the more they would produce. The more they produced, the more they would earn.

For Lloyd, this is where the fundamental systemic tension emerged. If all the herders acted in their individual best interest, the common resource (land) would be significantly depleted or even destroyed to the detriment of all, including the individual maximizing his or her best interest.

To put it more bluntly, when everyone does what is best for themselves, everyone can end up losing.

The Prisoners' Dilemma

"Game Theory" is a branch of mathematics that looks at competitive situations where the outcome of a participant's choice of action critically depends on the actions of other participants.

In this way, game theory is a great way of thinking about individual behavior within the Tragedy of the Commons.

For example, the classic game theory scenario called the Prisoner's Dilemma analyzes the decision matrix of two criminal accomplices who are interrogated separately by the police. Each criminal has two options: keep quiet or testify against their accomplice.

If they both keep quiet, they both receive a minor sentence but escape long-term incarceration. If they both testify against each other, they both receive a significant sentence. If only one person testifies against the other, the confessor goes free and the other person gets the most severe sentence.

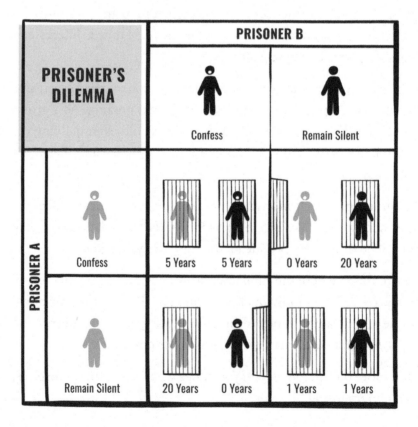

As an individual, the best option is to testify against the accomplice and thus go completely free. However, if both individuals pursue their best interests, they both get a significant sentence.

Therefore, the optimal solution is for both individuals to pursue their collective best interest. They must both commit to cooperate with each other by remaining silent. While they will both suffer slightly, ultimately they avoid the longest sentences.

Interestingly, for local communities, investing to solve homelessness poses a very similar dilemma.

To Invest or Not to Invest

Because of insufficiently coordinated and enforced state and federal strategies for ending homelessness, the thousands of city, town, and county governments across our country are each independently responsible for addressing homelessness in their own local way.

To dramatically oversimplify, each community has two strategic options:

- **Option A.** Attempt to house and provide services for everyone who is homeless.

- **Option B.** Do not provide housing and services and instead redirect people to other communities that do.

There are two big reasons why local leaders do not pursue Option A:

1. The cost of providing housing and services is substantial (especially without sufficient state and federal support).

2. There is a pervasive belief that most people who are homeless are not local (they became homeless somewhere else and then moved to the community). This belief signals an assumption that other communities have already selected Option B.

As a local leader, if I invest in homeless services and no one else does, our community will be overwhelmed by people seeking help (the most severe sentence).

If, however, I can guarantee that every community steps up a little bit (including my own), we will all have to contribute something, but together we will mount a more effective response.

INSIGHT #7	Local communities often perceive it to be in their selfish, short-term interest to do as little as possible to solve homelessness, which ends up hurting them in the long-term.

Local vs. Non-Local

The prisoner's dilemma, and Tragedy of the Commons more generally, is an extremely powerful systemic pattern, yet when it comes to homelessness, the decision not to act is almost always based on faulty logic.

As I just mentioned, in communities all across the country, there is a pervasive belief that people experiencing homelessness are "not from" the community where they are currently unhoused.

If there is anywhere to examine the "local" vs. "non-local" question, it is the San Francisco Bay Area. As one of the most liberal, progressive, and service-rich parts of the country, not to mention having fantastic year-round weather, the Bay Area would seemingly be an epicenter for nationwide homelessness.

Seven of the nine Bay Area counties do, in fact, track the origin of an individual's homelessness in their Point-in-Time Counts. The results will probably surprise you.

In these counties, 70-87% of people report that they were already living in that county when they became homeless.[3]

In fact, long-term data from the State of California has shown that 96% of people experiencing homelessness only access services in one community.[4]

Given these statistics, I am always surprised by how certain community members are that the revolving faces they see on the street are people from other communities.

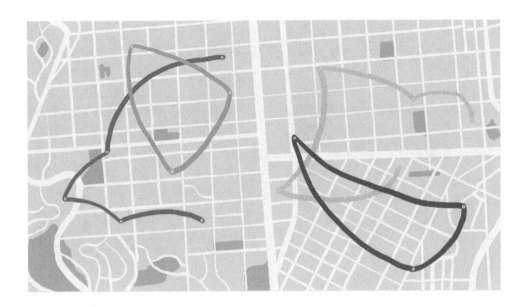

Rather than people moving from one community to another, it is much more common to see movement *within* a community.

This was evidenced by an amazing, year-long story in the *San Francisco Chronicle* called "Seven Lives, Seven Paths, Little Change Seen." As the City of San Francisco cracked down on unsheltered homelessness in one neighborhood, people simply shifted to a different neighborhood.[5]

From each neighborhood's perspective, it appeared that there were constantly new faces, but if you zoomed out even slightly, it was easy to see it was the same people moving within the same city.

Of course, it's also fair to ask, "So what if people are moving?"

I'll never forget a San Rafael City Council meeting when one council member expressed fear of this alleged "magnet effect" of providing new resources. They started suggesting we require people to show their high school yearbook pictures if they wanted to receive local services.

The Mayor had to jump in to remind his colleague, "There is something called the Constitution. This is a free country and people are allowed to move around."

Whether it's fleeing domestic violence or trying to connect with distant friends or family, sometimes people simply need a fresh start.

Chapter 16:
Hitting Rock Bottom in Marin

I started working in Marin County in the summer of 2013. As I've mentioned previously, Marin is the suburban community immediately north of the Golden Gate Bridge.

From the outside, Marin seems like the perfect place to try to solve homelessness.

- With a median household income of over $115,000, it is one of the wealthiest counties in the country.[1] This would suggest there could be significant resources available for services.

- It is extremely politically liberal (in 2020, 82.33% of Marinites voted for Joe Biden for president), which would suggest underlying support for issues like homelessness.[2]

- There are hundreds of thousands of acres of undeveloped land, which would suggest a significant number of places to create new housing.

Of course, as we have learned throughout this book, these surface-level factors are in fact the very issues, in many cases, exacerbating The Modern Homelessness Crisis.

SYSTEMIC FACTOR	CONDITIONS IN MARIN
Lack of Buildable Land for Housing	Almost 85% of the land in the county is protected for agricultural or parks.[3]
Single Family Zoning	Over 80% of the residential land in 9 of the county's 11 cities is restricted to single family zoning.[4]
Housing Regulation and NIMBYism	Politically liberal states and communities like California tend to have more highly regulated markets. NIMBYs are able to use this regulation to block more housing.
Lack of SROs and Flexible Housing Stock	Marin lacks cheap, studio units like SROs.
Affordable Housing Funding	Like communities across the country, Marin has historically lacked State and Federal funding for affordable housing.
Rent Burdened	In Marin, 63% of extremely low income renters (earning less than 30% of their area median income) are severely rent burdened, paying more than 50% of their income on rent.[5]
Redlining and Segregated Housing	Following WWII and an influx of Black Americans to support ship-building efforts, Marin saw redlining and racial restrictions throughout the county. Today, Black Marinites are 800% more likely to experience homelessness than they should.[6]
Unequal Opportunity	Even though legalized discrimination is outlawed, underlying patterns of segregation still impact opportunity in Marin. As recently as 2019, the State of California had to order a local school district to integrate students.[7]
Lack of Mental Health Beds	Like the rest of California, Marin lost the overwhelming majority of its long-term mental health beds due to deinstitutionalization.
Rates of Substance Abuse	Despite steady, statewide reductions in underage alcohol and drug use over the last decade, Marin County has seen increasing rates of substance use among young people.[8]

What is so powerful about systems thinking is that it provides a framework for seeing how all of these seemingly unrelated issues are actually inextricably linked.

No one is actively trying to create or perpetuate homelessness in Marin, but these underlying factors make it inevitable. As recently as 2017, Marin County had the seventh highest per capita rate of homelessness in the entire country.[9]

A Failed Response

When I started working in Marin, I had an intuitive sense of some of these issues, but I was primarily focused on running my own program. If we could just get more resources, I kept telling myself, then we could finally solve this crisis once and for all.

But then a strange thing happened. As the years ticked by, we did get more resources, and we helped more and more people, but the problem kept getting worse. It got worse quantitatively (our Point-in-Time Count kept going up), but the bigger problem seemed to be qualitative. It *looked* worse.

By 2015, San Rafael (Marin's largest city and where most of the county's homelessness issues were perceived to be) was reaching a boiling point.

As just one example: a local community member had begun sending *daily* emails to a list of about a thousand local residents, business owners, and public leaders decrying the state of homelessness in the community. These emails often included graphic pictures of human waste in front of businesses, descriptions of erratic and unsettling behavior stemming from behavioral health issues, and anecdotes of people being harassed or otherwise accosted by people in the homeless community.

I will *never* condone the tone and demeaning nature of these emails (this person would often refer to people experiencing homelessness as "urban terrorists") or the fact that this person would seek out and follow people to get pictures and reactions. However, there was, sadly, a truth to it.

Homelessness in San Rafael *had* gotten out of control.

The streets were filthy. Vibrant commercial areas were impacted. Throughout the county, it was common to hear people say they didn't go to Downtown San Rafael anymore because of all the homelessness.

Resources were being spent, but it wasn't resulting in people regaining housing. One study around that time found that long-term alcoholics in the homeless community were costing over $60,000 per person per year in public services (through emergency room visits, ambulance transports, criminal justice involvement, or other emergency services).[10]

All of this frustration started spurring action. Petitions were circulated. Community members started showing up in large numbers at public meetings. Local leaders were being compelled to act.

However, the substance of all of this activism was important. It illustrated just how deeply San Rafael and Marin had fallen into the predictable "hopeless" response to homelessness.

Like communities all across the country, Marin's anchor homeless service providers – a soup kitchen, an emergency shelter provider, and a day service center – had emerged in the 1970s and '80s.

While these organizations had always faced some level of community opposition, by 2015 it had reached a fever pitch, and all of the nuance around a complex issue like homelessness had been distilled to the singular question of whether a particular service provider should or should not be allowed to operate.

The activist I just mentioned was one of the leading voices calling for the organization's removal. In fact, he felt very strongly that *all* service providers should be shut down and Marin's homeless community should be relocated to a new service campus in neighboring Sonoma County.

This moment, this argument, was the pinnacle of abdicating responsibility and failing to effectively respond to this crisis.

Part 4:
Solutions

Chapter 17:
The Most Visible and Vulnerable

When it comes to any problem, especially a systemic one, I have become a firm believer in the proverbial wisdom of "measuring twice and cutting once."

For The Modern Homelessness Crisis, the vast majority of this book has been exactly that – diagnosing its most significant underlying causes.

In Part 1, we began with an overview of systems thinking and how it can help unpack complex issues like homelessness.

In Part 2, we used the systems thinking toolkit to create a map of the nationwide socioeconomic trends making homelessness more likely to occur, especially in major metropolitan areas.

Finally, in Part 3, we looked at some of the ineffective ways in which local communities have responded to the homelessness produced by the challenges identified in Part 2.

If you've made it this far, I am assuming you haven't lost faith that ending homelessness is possible, but I am also willing to bet that all of these high-level, systemic dynamics make the task feel nearly impossible.

As we came to learn in Marin County, this sense of overwhelm is actually an important step in the process.

In 2015, our local system of care was helping thousands of people every year, but both quantitatively and qualitatively, homelessness kept getting worse. In our frustration, we found ourselves forced to accept an uncomfortable but glaring truth: homelessness in our community had become unmanageable, and we did not know how to solve it.

Amazingly, this acceptance was the turning point. It gave us permission to begin looking beyond ourselves for solutions.

A History Changing Field Trip

In the summer of 2015, I was 100% invested in San Rafael's service center debate, and I thought I had the solution.

During part of the time I worked in Silicon Valley, I was based at a site called the Opportunity Center in Palo Alto, CA. The Opportunity Center (or "OC" as it was affectionately called) was the epitome of one-stop services for people in need.

When I first started volunteering and eventually working to end homelessness, it was through a program called Project Homeless Connect (PHC). PHC is like a job fair on steroids. In addition to prospective employers, it includes medical providers, housing locators, benefits coordinators, food, and more.

The core insight underlying PHC is that people experiencing homelessness spend huge portions of their days trying to use their limited resources to travel all across a community in order to access different services. This dynamic makes it even harder for people to exit homelessness because they're too busy with basic outputs (getting a meal, taking a shower, washing their clothes, finding somewhere to sleep) to focus on outcomes like securing employment or permanent housing.

By comparison, the best multi-service centers (like the OC) are essentially permanent PHCs. They bring all of these resources – food, hygiene, medical, and social services – under one roof. In the OC's case, it even included 90 units of on-site permanent housing.

As described in the last chapter, San Rafael had three different service providers located within two miles of each other:

- A shelter

- A soup kitchen

- A day services center (e.g., showers, medical services, case management)

As the debate raged in San Rafael about the location and impact of these local service providers, I started feeling like the OC might be the answer. Not only was it an opportunity to stitch all of these services together in one location, the OC even had an on-site garden and recreation area, which provided people with a safe and dignified place to spend their days.

With this vision in mind, I reached out to local City Councilmembers, County Supervisors, and nonprofit and business leaders to organize a field trip to Palo Alto so they could see the OC for themselves.

An Unexpected Discovery

When the group reconvened to debrief the trip, I expected everyone to rave about the OC and champion it as the solution to all of our challenges. While the group did almost universally love the facility, a nagging question dominated the discussion: if we built our own version of the Opportunity Center, would it actually solve the problems that the community was so concerned about, like loitering, trash, and disruptive behavior?

During our tour, we had in fact shared these concerns with senior staff from the organization that runs the OC. To our surprise, they nodded along and told us that just a few years earlier they had launched a program in San Mateo, CA, called the Homeless Outreach Team (HOT) to address those exact challenges.

Let me pause for a moment and note that there are only so many ways to slice and dice the words "homeless" and "outreach," so many communities have something called a "Homeless Outreach Team." This is a perfect example of the lack of credentialing and standardization that we discussed in Chapter 14. Having the same name does not necessarily indicate having the same program.

HOT in San Mateo was actually the brainchild of the local police department, which had reached its wits end with homelessness.

As discussed in Chapter 13, many communities use their police department as a tool for pushing homelessness out of their community (or 9 times out of 10, to another part of the same community). The San Mateo Police Department got tired of doing this.

Instead, they had a critical realization. It wasn't every single person experiencing homelessness that required their response. Instead, it was a small minority who were producing weekly or even daily contacts.

Most of the time, these contacts were for so-called "quality of life" issues, which rarely go anywhere in the court system. For low level offenses like drug possession, public intoxication, trespassing, and/or disorderly conduct, someone might spend a brief amount of time in jail, but they'd be back to the exact same spot within a few days or weeks. For most of these folks, this had been the dynamic *for years*.

Frustrated by this revolving door from the courts back to the streets, the San Mateo Police Department put together a list of the dozen most visible, disruptive, resource-intensive individuals in the city. Then, using their positional power in the community, they convened every local nonprofit and delivered the following challenge: if we can't leverage the collective knowledge and resources of all of the organizations in our community to permanently house these dozen people, then seriously, what are we doing?

There wasn't a clear path forward, but the group pledged to start meeting every two weeks while maintaining an exclusive focus on developing permanent housing opportunities for the people on the list (i.e., permanently resolving their homelessness).

Slowly but surely, this approach started working. By the time we met them in 2015, about five years into the process, San Mateo had housed nearly all of the most visible and vulnerable people experiencing homelessness in their downtown. They had even expanded the methodology to other communities throughout the county.

Different Community, Same Problem

As our debrief continued back in San Rafael, we gradually realized we were facing the same dilemma. A small minority of our overall homeless community was generating the vast majority of community complaints and calls for service.

- 90% of visibly homeless people (i.e., people we knew by name through different local service providers) had ZERO interaction with the fire department[1]

- 60% had ZERO interaction with the police department[2]

Similar figures have been observed all across the country. And in some extreme cases, such as the infamous case of "Million Dollar Murray," communities can literally spend millions of dollars on emergency interventions for a single individual experiencing homelessness.[3]

Beyond the societal impact, however, morally, we would eventually learn that people experiencing this type of long-term, high-impact homelessness are some of the most vulnerable people in the community. In fact, on average, people experiencing long-term homelessness die 20+ years earlier than their housed peers, primarily from untreated chronic illnesses.[4]

SERVICE UTILIZATION

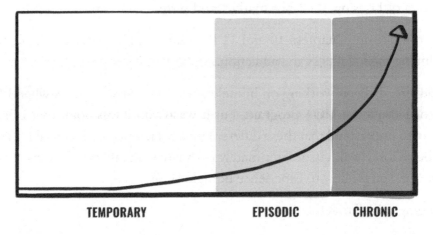

| TEMPORARY | EPISODIC | CHRONIC |

Amazingly, just like in San Mateo, in San Rafael our local service providers and law enforcement officials knew all of these people by name. They were very rarely new to the community. Instead, they had been homeless and receiving local services for years, in some cases decades.

As the months went by, we continued meeting and sharing the stories of the most vulnerable people in our community, and as this happened, we gradually began to reframe our core problem.

We didn't need a new service center. We needed a new strategy for serving people experiencing *chronic homelessness*.

Chronic Homelessness

This book opened with a paradox, which we began to unpack in Chapter 10 with the concept of "chronic homelessness."

On one hand, data shows that there is rapid turnover and self-resolution in the homeless community, yet at the same time, our experience of homelessness tends to be dominated by memorable encounters with people who are extremely vulnerable and seem to have been homeless for a very long time.

In Part 2, we learned that there are multiple factors that increase the likelihood that someone will become homeless.

Chapters 7, 8, and 9 focused on some of the biggest financial factors, such as the cost of housing, the labor market, and systemic racism.

By comparison, Chapters 10 and 11 focused on behavioral health factors, including mental illness and addiction.

I had already been working on homelessness for nearly six years when I first learned about the HOT program, but it wasn't until this point that I finally began to understand that these different inflow factors (i.e., financial hardship vs. behavioral health issues) ultimately correlate with different lengths of time that a person is likely to experience homelessness.

Bringing this all together:

- For the vast majority of people who experience homelessness, it is a relatively brief experience that is overwhelmingly caused by a financial or relational crisis (an eviction, job loss, rent increase, health crisis, domestic violence, divorce).

- By comparison, for the 10-30% of the overall homeless community that is experiencing long-term, chronic homelessness, the overwhelming majority are suffering from significant disabling conditions (mental illness, addiction, traumatic brain injury, chronic health issues).

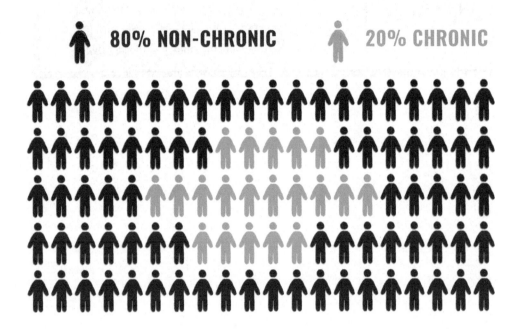

These different causes and durations of homelessness help to explain one of the biggest tensions communities all across the country experience when they try to respond to The Modern Homelessness Crisis.

It can be quantitatively true that the service providers in a homeless system of care can house hundreds, if not thousands, of people every year while conditions on the street barely change or even get worse.

This is because most housing placements are among people who are part of the short-term, financially impacted group of people experiencing homelessness; whereas, people experiencing long-term, chronic homelessness do not receive the support they desperately need.

Ironically, and quite tragically, it is often the significant community impacts from people experiencing chronic homelessness, who again by definition are people with serious disabilities, that make policymakers – and the public at-large – less likely to want to help this specific subpopulation.

That was certainly the case in Marin, until HOT gave us a new path forward.

INSIGHT #8	Solving The Modern Homelessness Crisis requires addressing two different problems: providing short-term assistance for people who experience financial shocks and providing long-term care for people suffering from disabling health conditions.

Chapter 18:
One Person at a Time

Inspired by our field trip to Palo Alto, the Homeless Outreach Team (HOT) in San Mateo, and everything we were learning about chronic homelessness, in February of 2016, our team in Marin decided to launch our own version of HOT, initially focused on the dozen or so most visible, vulnerable, chronically homeless people in Downtown San Rafael.

A New Way of Working Together

Just like the San Mateo program, our HOT pilot started with an official challenge from an official source – the City of San Rafael and the County of Marin.

That alone was a big lift.

All across the country, I repeatedly see the same dynamic. Cities (which usually possess "reactive" tools like police, fire, and public works departments) are busy arguing with counties (which usually possess health and human service functions) over who is truly responsible for addressing homelessness. Cities say counties should play a bigger role because of their social service capacity. Counties, which serve much larger geographic areas, don't feel the same on-the-ground impact as cities, so they feel that cities should do more to increase local resources.

In hindsight, by including city *and* county leaders on our field trips (we took many more to other local jurisdictions after learning so much in San Mateo) and by learning about chronic homelessness and different ways to address it *together*, we began forming relationships that did not previously exist. As a result, the City and the County became willing to partner in a way that they had not been in the past.

I also have to give a huge amount of credit to our local service providers, including the St. Vincent de Paul Society of Marin, the Ritter Center, Homeward Bound of Marin, and the Marin Housing Authority.

Government agencies are often stuck at the policy and funding level. Service providers, on the other hand, are the ones doing the actual work. Fortunately, because our providers were also included in these learning sessions, they too felt buy-in to try something different. Indeed, they were some of the biggest advocates for change.

Once we all got in the room together, that's when the magic really happened.

More than anything, HOT is a process and methodology for effective case conferencing, which is a fancy way of saying "coordinating services for the people our programs serve."

Over the years, our team identified four aspects of this process that made it so successful, the first three of which we'll discuss in this chapter:

1. Strong project management

2. An exclusive focus on housing

3. Taking a systems view

#1: Strong Project Management

A common mistake in the social service sector – and many other sectors for that matter – is asking people to do work they aren't trained to do. For example, businesses don't ask accountants to work on the marketing team, and universities don't ask professors to process financial aid applications.

In the social service sector, social workers (often called "case managers") are fantastic at helping vulnerable people articulate and achieve their goals.

However, they might not be as skilled at project management.

Project management is the process of leading the work of a team to achieve a goal or objective. HOT requires strong project management, and for us, that meant:

- Coordinating a bi-weekly meeting

- Taking detailed meeting notes and minutes

- Facilitating participation from everyone in the group

- Developing and assigning action items during meetings

- Following up on action items between meetings

We were extremely fortunate to have a former tech executive, Howard Schwartz, join our team around that time. Howard had begun volunteering and eventually working with the St. Vincent de Paul Society of Marin, and as he got involved with HOT, we were able to leverage his project management background to drive our work in a truly unprecedented way.

#2: Housing Outcomes

Next, HOT required a new perspective on outcomes – specifically, permanent housing placements.

I have participated in a lot of case conferencing discussions over the years, and they are typically just "update" meetings where different agencies (or staff within one agency) chat about the latest happenings with their clients.

In update meetings, there are also actions and efforts to "connect people with services," but in my experience, it's rarely about permanent housing. Instead, it might look like:

- Person X just got released from jail. How do we get them into temporary shelter?

- Person Y is newly homeless in our community. How do we register them for benefits?

- Person Z is causing problems for a downtown business. Can someone go talk to them and ask them to move to another area?

This can feel like progress until you take a step back and realize the same people are simply churning through the system year after year, not getting the help they truly need (i.e., a permanent roof over their heads).

By comparison, with HOT, we became laser-focused on three goals:

1. Are we working with the people who have the highest needs?

2. Are we getting them housed?

3. Are they staying housed?

These goals drove everything we did, and as we saw all the way back in Chapter 2, goals are the foundation of any system.

#3: A Systems View

The next component, which I believe was a unique contribution of our iteration in San Rafael, was to take a systems perspective.

A lot of case conferencing meetings involve frontline social workers. This makes sense because they have the most direct knowledge about clients; however, HOT also included senior leadership from local service providers, the City, and the County.

This was absolutely key.

The first half of our HOT meeting was focused on a small number of individual people (10-15 max). During that time, we developed actionable steps toward getting each individual closer to permanent housing.

The second half of the meeting, however, was focused on "the system." During that portion, we discussed common barriers that were preventing progress toward housing for multiple people.

Interestingly, many of these common barriers seemed to originate from the fact that one part of the system did not fully understand how best to utilize services from another part of the system. Thus, these discussions were often designed as presentations from partner agencies who could provide an overview about how their programs and services worked (e.g., entry requirements, legal regulations, funding constraints).

Fortunately, the launch of HOT coincided with the graduate school class I mentioned at the very beginning of this book, "Reimagining Slums." As I started learning about systems thinking in that class, I decided to try to capture the insights from our HOT meetings on a systems map.

This map, and the insights we gleaned from it, ended up being critically important for embracing the fourth and final element of the HOT program: Housing First.

Chapter 19:
Housing First

Thanks to the Homeless Outreach Team program (HOT), our community finally had a forum to begin to unpack the complexity of our local homeless system of care (and why it was failing to deliver results for our most vulnerable community members).

To keep track of everything we were learning during our discussions, I volunteered to create a visual.

Every two weeks after one of our HOT meetings, I would go back to my office and put up new sticky notes (elements) and draw new arrows (interconnections) trying to incorporate everything we were learning.

As I continued hanging up new drafts of the map, my co-workers glibly began referring to it as "the wall of misery."

Homelessness was eventually denoted in the very middle of the map and long-term housing was on the outside. There were a lot of arrows connecting a lot of services toward the middle of the map, but very few paths led to permanent housing.

A Vicious Cycle

There was always an intuitive sense among our service providers that we weren't coordinating as well as we could, but our systems map brought the reality into sharper focus.

Despite the best of intentions over nearly four decades, this was Marin's "Homeless Industrial Complex."

- Nonprofits and government departments were working in silos.

- We lacked effective cross-agency communication.

- We weren't implementing best practices.

The sum result, as my co-workers had observed, was that vulnerable people were not getting the help they desperately needed.

Importantly, as we continued refining our map, we began to see the reason why.

Over the years, our system of care had unintentionally created an extremely powerful feedback loop that was actually *perpetuating* chronic homelessness.

This feedback loop became increasingly evident as we started identifying patterns among people who had been experiencing chronic homeless in Marin for 10, 20, even 30+ years.

In short:

- People experiencing chronic homelessness, who by definition have disabling conditions that make it harder for them to resolve their homelessness, were consistently "failing out of" or being terminated from local programs.

- These program terminations, in turn, lowered people's faith that the system could deliver results, which then caused them not to seek help.

- As people (understandably) withdrew and became skeptical of local services, their underlying conditions continued to get worse, making it even harder to serve them if they did decide to re-engage.

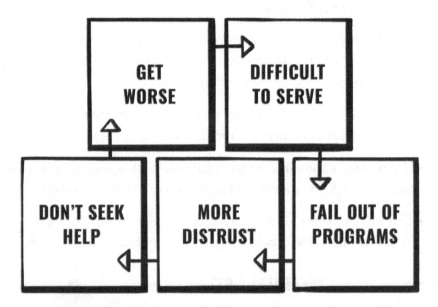

Treatment First

The chronic homeless feedback loop that we discovered in Marin County is playing out in many communities, and it is one of the biggest reasons why chronic homelessness has become so entrenched all across the country.

Importantly, the origin of this feedback loop points to one of the most critical insights of the entire book – indeed, of systems thinking generally.

When it comes to changing any system, the most powerful lever of all has nothing to do with programs, policies, laws, or even institutions.

Instead, it is the recognition that *human systems are ultimately predicated on human beliefs and assumptions*.

As writer and philosopher Robert Pirsig once observed:

If a factory is torn down but the rationality that produced it is left standing, then that rationality will simply produce another factory. If a revolution destroys a government, but the systematic patterns of thought that produced that government are left intact, then those patterns will repeat themselves … there's so much talk about the system. And so little understanding.[1]

While our systems map undeniably revealed siloed inefficiency, it also visualized a powerful assumption at the root of how many communities in the United States respond to homelessness.

If someone loses their housing, many providers and policymakers believe that before that person can regain housing, they must *first* address the underlying reason(s) they became homeless. For example:

- If someone becomes homeless because of economic circumstances, then they should get another job, and then they'll get housing.

- If someone is homeless because of mental illness, then they should seek treatment for that mental illness, and then they'll get housing.

- If someone is homeless because of a health or developmental issue, then they should seek help for that issue, and then they'll get housing.

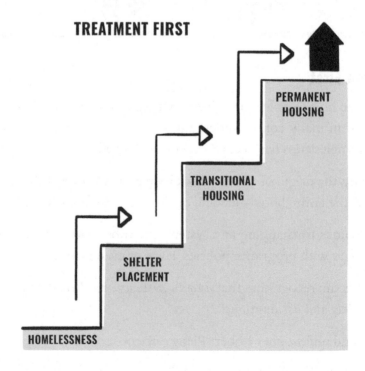

TREATMENT FIRST

PERMANENT HOUSING

TRANSITIONAL HOUSING

SHELTER PLACEMENT

HOMELESSNESS

In other words, the assumption is that homelessness should be addressed with "Treatment First," which typically means offering increasingly stable housing options (emergency shelter then transitional housing then permanent housing) as a person demonstrates progress toward employability, sobriety, treatment, etc.

On one hand, this logic makes sense. In fact, haven't I spent most of this book talking about the importance of getting to root causes?

Indeed, in practice, this service strategy does work for a lot of people, though I would argue it primarily works for the people who are already highly likely to resolve their homelessness (i.e., people experiencing short-term, financially-driven homelessness).

Unfortunately, however, as our team in Marin started to discover as we began mapping the experiences of people in our system, at every interim step between homelessness and permanent housing, seemingly logical program requirements (such as sobriety, having a path to increasing income, being compliant with mental health medications) were causing people (especially chronically homeless people) to fail out of our programs, thus returning to the street before they were permanently housed.

Housing First

As always, Iain De Jong has a helpful analogy for thinking about what we were witnessing.

Imagine you're having a heart attack. Your family is terrified. They call 911. An ambulance comes to your house and rushes you to the hospital. When you get to the emergency room, the medics roll you into an operating room. You are at death's door, and then your doctor says:

> Oh, it's you. You know, we have been talking about your heart condition. I told you to start exercising and to eat more fruits and vegetables. Let's do this: I'm going to discharge you. Go home and eat vegan for six weeks. Also try to jog for 30–60 minutes 3–5 times per week. Oh, and don't forget to stop smoking. Once you've done that, come back to the emergency room, and then we'll see about treating your heart attack.[2]

If this response sounds ridiculous, it should. The healthcare industry learned a long time ago that to address root cause conditions, it is sometimes imperative to solve the crisis first – all judgment aside.

Indeed, as early as the 1990s, practitioners began questioning the Treatment First philosophy. One of the most notable early mavericks was Sam Tsemberis from Pathways Housing in New York City.

Rather than requiring all the hallmarks of Treatment First – sobriety, compliance with prescribed medications, or employment – Tsembersis began experimenting with offering chronically homeless people unconditional permanent *housing first*. Once inside, the person was then offered intensive wraparound support services, which were designed to stabilize the underlying issues that led to that person's homelessness.

As counterintuitive as this model might initially seem, over the past 25+ years, the "Housing First" model has now been replicated all across the country, and the results are unequivocal. In community after community, from Salt Lake City, UT, to Bergen County, NJ, to Marin County, CA, studies have found that Housing First is up to five times more effective than Treatment First at ensuring long-term housing retention for people experiencing chronic homelessness.[3]

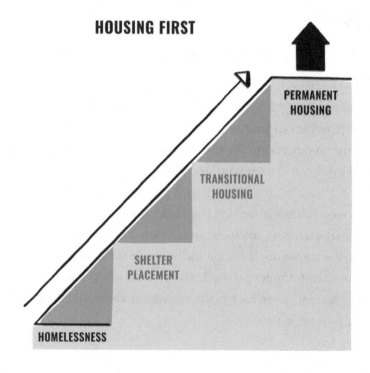

HOUSING FIRST

PERMANENT HOUSING

TRANSITIONAL HOUSING

SHELTER PLACEMENT

HOMELESSNESS

Between rental subsidies and case management services, implementing Housing First can be resource intensive, but remember the alternative. By keeping people housed and reducing their public service utilization, Housing First can be more than 50% cheaper than letting people languish on the streets.

Morally and economically, it has proven to be the most effective intervention.

What Housing First Is Actually Solving

As we observed in Chapter 14, when ideas like Housing First emerge and start to spread, there is no inherent accountability structure to dictate how and where they are used.

As a consequence, as Housing First has gained more traction across the country (and the world), it has gone from a specific housing program in New York City to, in some cases, an entire philosophy or strategy for how communities respond to homelessness.

In many ways this is great. For example, it moves our country closer to the idea that *housing is a human right*, and a permanent placement – independent of preconditions – should be our first offer for someone who has become homeless.

At the same time, some people seem to conflate the "harm reduction" aspects of Housing First (e.g., not requiring strict sobriety for program participants) with broader public policy debates about criminal justice, homelessness, and what types of rules communities should or should not enforce around public intoxication and other "quality of life" issues.

Ultimately, I think these discussions distract us from seeing what Housing First is really capable of achieving.

At the end of Chapter 18, we saw that solving The Modern Homelessness Crisis requires addressing two different problems: providing short-term assistance for people who experience financial shocks and providing long-term care for people suffering from disabling health conditions.

This latter problem, long-term care for disabling health conditions, has its origins in what we learned in Chapter 10 about deinstitutionalization. As long-term, residential hospitals were shut down in the 1960s and 1970s, nothing was implemented in their place, and many extremely vulnerable people simply ended up on the street.

In my view, the original iteration of Housing First – a housing placement strategy for people experiencing chronic homelessness – is finally the community-based mental health treatment that was promised during deinstitutionalization but was never actually delivered. It is the way for people with complex health needs, particularly behavioral health challenges, to be fully integrated and supported in community-based settings.

INSIGHT #9	Housing First is the answer for providing long-term care for people suffering from disabling health conditions.

HOT Starts Heating Up

As we began working to house people in San Rafael through HOT, those housing placements ultimately took the form of Housing First. We cobbled together rental subsidies, provided intensive wraparound services, and offered people the chance to come back inside.

Amazingly, it started to work.

Over the first 18 months of piloting this new approach to chronic homelessness, we housed 23 of the most vulnerable, visible, high-impact individuals in the downtown area. These were people who had been homeless in our community for decades.

With this success, we began to wonder – could this methodology become the basis for our entire countywide system of care?

Chapter 20:
Coordinated Entry

In the late spring of 2011, during my final months with AmeriCorps VISTA, I was asked to coordinate our biggest Project Homeless Connect (PHC) yet – an 80-vendor event at San Jose's City Hall.

Over the preceding twelve months I had tried to move away from large, bi-annual PHCs based in San Jose (a community already rich in services) to smaller, more frequent events in underserved neighboring communities like Gilroy, Milpitas, and Sunnyvale.

This model seemed to be working. In just a few months we had doubled annual attendance.

I didn't mind the logistics of hosting another mega-event. Instead, I had serious reservations about the intent – local leaders wanted to use PHC to administer a survey.

At that time, Santa Clara County was just about to start a new campaign called "Housing 1000," which had the goal of permanently housing one thousand of the most vulnerable people experiencing long-term homelessness.

While I certainly wasn't opposed to housing one thousand people, the approach and rationale didn't make any sense to me.

At that time, I thought PHC worked because it brought together as many different service providers as possible, each of whom could offer prospective clients their own proprietary assessments and services to address people's unique needs. Why would we want to create a universal, countywide survey that seemed to overrule the expertise of these individual agencies? And, more importantly, why would we make housing placements contingent on the results of that survey?

It would take me another six years to change my mind.

Triage

In the last chapter, I shared Iain de Jong's emergency room analogy for Housing First. When it comes to solving homelessness, Iain and many others believe this healthcare comparison should be applied even more broadly.

Think about what happens when a person is having a medical emergency, like a heart attack, and they need to go to the hospital. Over many decades, hospitals across the world have developed a fairly standardized and consistent system for determining and addressing patient needs:

- If we get really sick, we go to a centralized location within the hospital called the emergency room.

- Within the emergency room, a nurse or doctor triages our symptoms and needs with a standardized assessment.

- Based on the results of that assessment, hospital staff route us to the medical intervention we need, while also indicating how urgently that intervention should to be applied.

This probably sounds so obvious it's hard to imagine an alternative, but consider a different process.

What if we had to go to the hospital, but there was no central check-in location and no emergency room? Instead, what if we had to go department by department, wasting valuable time completing different forms and surveys to see if we're in the right place.

As a patient this would be extremely frustrating, but it would also be a headache for the hospital. Unless all of those different departments were regularly coordinating and sharing data, they would have no idea who was seeking services and what types of assistance those people needed.

In this inefficient system, we can easily imagine extremely vulnerable people wandering through the halls, trying to get the help they desperately need without actually knowing where to go. In fact, they might get so frustrated that they reject this system all together and refuse to engage in further care.

Sadly, this hypothetical sounds very similar to the way many communities have historically approached homelessness:

- Every agency has its own unique process and approach.

- Care is not effectively coordinated across agencies.

- Valuable time and energy is wasted trying to navigate the system.

- The most vulnerable get lost in the shuffle, often becoming more distrustful of the system and more fragile in the process.

Coordinated Entry

Beginning in the 2010s, federal agencies like the Department of Housing and Urban Development (HUD) and the Veterans Administration (VA) began requiring that communities become more coordinated in their provision of services.

This strategy is known as "Coordinated Entry."

[Coordinated Entry is] a framework that transforms a [local system of care] from a network of homeless assistance projects making individual decisions about whom to serve, into a fully integrated crisis response system. By gathering information through a standardized assessment process, coordinated entry provides a [community] and community partners with data that can be used for client level service linkages, system and project planning, and resource allocation. Historically, [communities] allowed each project to operate individually by developing and implementing their own admission criteria, assessment and eligibility screening, prioritization processes and enrollment decisions. CE orients the community to a standard set of prioritizing principles by which the community is able to make consistent decisions about how to utilize its resources most effectively. By having standardized processes, the system increases accessibility for clients; it is no longer about who the person happens to speak with on a given day or making a person fit into a program. Rather, it is about understanding and responding to the person's individualized needs.[1]

Building off our healthcare analogy, Coordinated Entry seeks to create the triaging process that takes place in hospitals:

- People experiencing homelessness complete a common assessment form.

- Because there is a common assessment, there is "no wrong door." Wherever someone enters the system (a shelter, a meal program, a health clinic), they are evaluated in the same way.

- The assessment helps indicate with some level of objectively how severe that person's needs are.

- Those needs then point to the type of housing intervention that is most likely to help that person permanently end their homelessness (e.g., short-term rental assistance or long-term supportive housing).

WITH COORDINATED ENTRY

DIFFERING LEVELS OF NEED

APPROPRIATE LEVEL OF SUPPORT

ACCESS ➔ ASSESS ➔ ASSIGN

Importantly, HUD requires that communities create Coordinated Entry systems, but it does not dictate all of the details of how these systems are operated. This lack of detailed oversight and credentialing means that Coordinated Entry can take many different forms, even across neighboring communities.

So, the question is, what's the most effective way to operate Coordinated Entry?

The First By-Name-List

In the mid-2000s, street homelessness in New York City had reached crisis levels.

For many years outreach workers had been walking the streets providing respite items like sandwiches and blankets to people in need. While this support was no doubt providing some degree of comfort, it wasn't resulting in people ending their homelessness.

Frustrated by the lack of movement to permanent housing, in 2004, the nonprofit organization Breaking Ground launched a program called "Street to Home" in Times Square. The effort, modeled after the "Rough Sleepers Initiative" in England, had a simple goal: target outreach to people with the longest histories of homelessness and then use Housing First to get them back inside.

Street to Home ended up being a resounding success with homelessness in the 20-block area around Times Square declining 87%.[2]

In addition to validating Housing First, this campaign introduced two new innovations: the idea of a "homeless registry" and the use of a "Vulnerability Index (VI)."

According to a report from the Urban Institute:

> The registry introduced the concept that street outreach workers should know the names, faces, homeless histories, and vulnerability factors of all people experiencing homelessness. The VI is the assessment tool used to collect this information.[3]

As one leader at the time put it:

> It's ridiculous to think that as a community you're making a serious go at addressing street homelessness if you don't have a proactive, consistent, methodical method of having a list of who's outside.[4]

Given the success in New York, other communities took notice and wanted to launch their own versions of the program.

In 2007, Los Angeles County Supervisor Zev Yaroslavsky launched Project 50. This pilot program aimed to house the 50 individuals living on Skid Row who had the greatest risk of dying on the streets.

To determine who was most vulnerable, local providers conducted a "Registry Week" whereby volunteers trained by Breaking Ground canvassed Skid Row to survey people living on the streets and in shelters using a VI. The people who completed these assessments were then prioritized based on "vulnerability" (i.e., how close they appeared to be to dying on the street).

Project 50 ultimately housed 67 of the most vulnerable people on Skid Row, providing yet another data point that communities can build by-name-list registries of the most vulnerable people and then use data to track housing placements from these lists.

Harnessing growing interest and momentum, in 2010, Breaking Ground launched the "100,000 Homes Campaign." This initiative was modeled after the 100,000 Lives Campaign, which had mobilized hospitals across the country to adopt evidence-based practices to save more lives.

In 2011, leadership from Breaking Ground formed a new nonprofit called Community Solutions, and Community Solutions took over running the campaign.

Like its healthcare counterpart, the 100,000 Homes Campaign was aimed at helping communities all across the country adopt evidence-based practices (registry weeks, vulnerability assessments, Housing First) to house people experiencing chronic homelessness.

What I did not fully appreciate going into my final Project Homeless Connect in 2011 was that Santa Clara County's "Housing 1,000" initiative was our community's local commitment toward the 100,000 Homes national goal. Yes, local leaders wanted to connect people with services at the event, but they really wanted to roll out these new strategies in order to prioritize vulnerable people experiencing chronic homelessness for housing opportunities.

By July 2014, thanks to the 100,000 Homes Campaign, 186 different communities across the country had successfully housed 105,580 people.[5]

Built for Zero

The 100,000 Homes Campaign was a monumental accomplishment, but surprisingly, it did not achieve Community Solutions' true vision – sizable reductions in the number of people experiencing homelessness.

In line with many of the insights in this book, Community Solutions would go on to acknowledge that:

Homelessness is a dynamic problem that cannot be solved with a fixed recipe. Like any complex problem, homelessness is a series of problems to be solved. New people experience it over time, and the phenomenon itself changes with the intersection of homelessness and other unpredictable events and conditions. The data and tools available to communities have been too slow and cumbersome to respond to such a rapidly changing problem.[6]

To address this dynamism, Community Solutions realized it needed to find a way to help homeless systems of care become more adaptive to the evolving nature of homelessness.

To that end, in 2015, they launched the Built for Zero Campaign:

Adequate resources, evidence-informed policy, and proven best practices like Housing First are crucial building blocks. But alone, they are merely the raw materials of an effective response to homelessness. It is the way communities put these building blocks together — the systems they design for integrating and rearranging them in response to a complex and constantly shifting problem — that determines who ends homelessness and who doesn't. We call this insight the Systems Problem, and if the 100,000 Homes Campaign helped us to surface it, we have designed Built for Zero … to help communities solve it.[7]

In essence, Built for Zero is an effort to create Coordinated Entry systems that more effectively respond to the way people "flow" in and out of the experience of homelessness. It does this in three important ways.

First, the Built for Zero campaign and organizations like Community Solutions are helping to reconceptualize what ending homelessness really means.

Functional zero is a dynamic milestone that indicates a community has solved homelessness for a population (e.g. people experiencing chronic homelessness, veterans). Reaching and sustaining this milestone is in service of building a future where homelessness is rare, brief, and nonrecurring.[8]

In practice, Functional Zero looks like housing every person experiencing chronic homelessness in a given community while preventing any new people from becoming chronically homeless. If a person does become chronically homeless (i.e., has remained unhoused for longer than a year), the system should be able to identify that person, rapidly provide supportive housing for them, and as a result, the overall number of people experiencing chronic homelessness should not increase.

To say this a slightly different way, the goal is to get to a point where a homeless system of care is able to house people faster than they are becoming homeless.

The ability to measure whether Functional Zero has been achieved is dependent on the second component of Built for Zero's work – facilitating "real time" data.

Communities that participate with this movement commit to reliably tracking homelessness across their entire geography, at least monthly and on a person-specific basis (i.e., through a by-name-list).

In essence, this type of Coordinated Entry system is creating a HOT Program across an entire jurisdiction. Outreach workers, service providers, and other community partners are actively convening, sharing data, and working together on clients that touch different parts of the system.

At its best, this approach helps communities move away from the mentality that Agency X helps these clients and Agency Y helps those clients to the perspective that every person experiencing homelessness is every agency's client, whether they directly serve them or not.

When a system of care reaches this point, it is able to embrace Built for Zero's third tenet: applying a quality improvement framework for systems change.

Rather than completely overhauling the way services are provided, Built for Zero's focus on quality improvement means communities implement small adjustments to the way programs are operated, they measure the results of those pilots, and they do more of what works and less of what doesn't.

As described above, these efforts are primarily focused on two major levers: reducing inflow and increasing outflow.

As just one example, many communities have some existing stock of supportive housing units. Thus, one strategy for increasing outflow is placing people in vacant units as quickly as possible.

| REDUCE INFLOW | $+$ | INCREASE OUTFLOW | $=$ | FUNCTIONAL ZERO |

This might seem somewhat trivial but consider the following. A 2022 investigative report in San Francisco found that the City had 888 *vacant* supportive housing units, and there were at least 400 individuals who had been waiting *over a year* to be placed in one of these units.[9] Simply filling all of those existing units would have reduced homelessness in San Francisco by an eighth.

Rather than completely redesigning this system, which would likely cause even longer delays, a quality improvement lens would challenge providers to make more rapid, marginal improvements. Can we go from twelve months to filling a unit to nine months, then nine months to six months, and so on?

By creating these new processes and accountability structures, Built for Zero helps communities effectively dismantle many aspects of the homeless industrial complex.

UNDERLYING CHALLENGE	BUILT FOR ZERO'S IMPACT
Silos	Requires multiple stakeholders to come together around a shared planning and accountability process.
Poor Data	Every community must provide monthly report outs on their progress. Data is used to improve systems.
Credentialing	The Built for Zero coalition coordinates training and coaching from national experts who can share what works and what doesn't.
Government Inaction	By building and promoting the work of the coalition, communities see that others are doing their part, thus making it easier for them to take action, too.

Measurable Results

Back in Marin County in early 2017, we were starting to have success with the HOT program and Housing First, but that was also the same time that Marin's per capita rate of homelessness reached the top ten nationwide.

Unless HOT was just going to be another boutique program that we could point to and say we were effectively *managing* homelessness, we had to make it more systemic.

Fortunately, it was around this time that our team discovered Built for Zero and their approach to Coordinated Entry. We immediately recognized that HOT's "by-name-list" was basically the same thing as Built for Zero's by-name-list. The only difference was that our list had been subjectively determined.

As we learned more about registry weeks and vulnerability assessments, we decided to roll these efforts out locally.

In the late summer of 2017, just like Housing 1000 back in 2011, we did a countywide push to survey people experiencing homelessness, which helped us to create a more objective by-name-list oriented around vulnerability.

We then continued to utilize Housing First, which was resolving homelessness for people we never thought would make it back inside.

Seeing this success locally, and becoming increasingly inspired by the successes in other Built for Zero communities, our strategic intent started to shift. We began moving away from "How can we effectively house people experiencing chronic homelessness?" and toward "How do we *solve* chronic homelessness?"

I cannot overstate the importance of alignment around this vision.

Through my role with the City, I helped co-found a working group with the horribly governmental name of the "Marin Chronic Homeless Action Task-force" (MCHAT). The idea was simple. To drive the systemic change needed to solve chronic homelessness, we needed to include:

- County leaders

- Leadership from cities and towns throughout the county

- Nonprofit service providers

- The business community

- Philanthropy

- Faith-based partners

Many communities engage in lengthy, costly, and ultimately ineffective strategic planning processes around homelessness. In Marin, we never had to do this.

Instead, through our growing coalition of local service providers, as well as MCHAT, which later rebranded itself as Opening Doors Marin, we built multi-sector alignment around the idea that every partner should be contributing what they could to the shared goal of ending chronic homelessness.

Because of this commitment, we essentially created a positive, reinforcing feedback loop. As partners began contributing new resources, we started housing more people, and these successes led to a willingness to contribute even more. Some examples included:

- The Marin Housing Authority committed housing vouchers for people experiencing chronic homelessness.

- The County of Marin funded a landlord recruitment program through the Marin Housing Authority to help ensure we could find rental opportunities for those housing vouchers.

- The County also pledged new case management resources to go with the vouchers.

- Service providers began hiring and training "Housing First" case managers.

- Cities and towns pooled funding to create even more case management.

- We leveraged new State and local philanthropic dollars to build new permanent supportive housing units.

- We implemented new data sharing and reporting policies to measure our impact and break down silos across organizations.

- Through offsites, social gatherings, and regular meetings, we made a genuine commitment to building relationships across agencies, so much so that we eventually started referring to our homeless system of care as our "one agency."

The results have been profound.

We officially launched our new "by-name-list" Coordinated Entry system on October 1, 2017, and within two years, our community was able to reduce chronic homelessness by 28%.

As of publishing this book, over 500 people experiencing chronic homelessness have been housed in Marin County, 94% of whom remain housed.[10]

These statistics have been mirrored or exceeded all across the country. As of March 2022, BFZ has seen:

- 12 communities end veteran homelessness,

- 5 communities end chronic homelessness,

- 63 communities achieve quality, real-time data on homelessness, and

- 49 communities use that data to demonstrate a measurable reduction in homelessness.[11]

Chapter 21:
Bringing It All Together

So far in Part 4 we have looked at some important building blocks for what a more effective response to homelessness should include, and I want to make sure it is clear how all of these different pieces can fit together.

To that end, I have created a new systems map called "STEP":

- S - Systems

- T - Triage

- E - Engagement

- P - Placement

This chapter will provide a high-level overview of STEP, but for an even more detailed breakdown, as well as resources for how you can use the STEP framework to evaluate homelessness programming in your community, please visit:

www.howtosolvehomelessness.org.

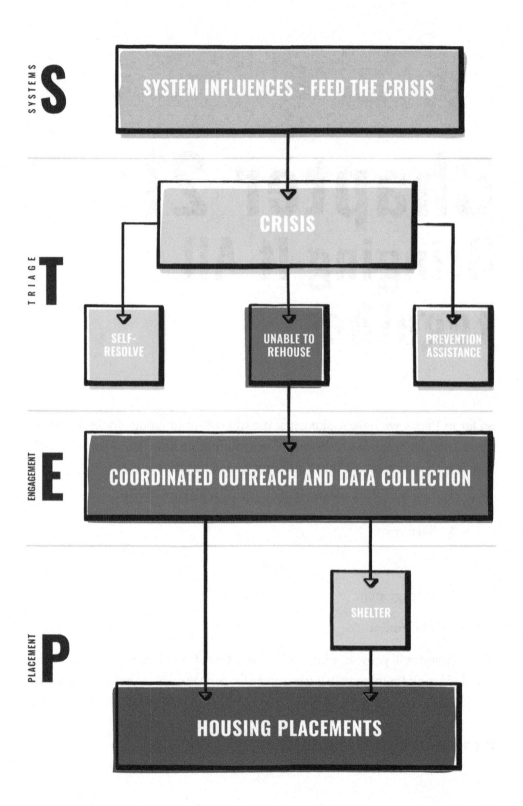

SYSTEMS **S**

SYSTEM INFLUENCES - FEED THE CRISIS

TRIAGE **T**

CRISIS

SELF-RESOLVE

UNABLE TO REHOUSE

PREVENTION ASSISTANCE

ENGAGEMENT **E**

COORDINATED OUTREACH AND DATA COLLECTION

PLACEMENT **P**

SHELTER

HOUSING PLACEMENTS

S - Systems

At its core, The Modern Homelessness Crisis is really a symptom of other problems – a lack of housing production, economic inequality, systemic racism, mental illness, and addiction.

Therefore, the most effective strategy for solving The Modern Homelessness Crisis is to reform these underlying systems, thus reducing the likelihood and severity of the types of crises that push people into homelessness.

The S in STEP acknowledges the importance of this frontend work, and Chapter 23 is dedicated to exploring systemic solutions for these upstream challenges.

T - Triage

Like homelessness overall, the most effective strategy for resolving a person's housing crisis is to prevent that person from becoming homeless in the first place.

Here we find the value of comparing homeless service systems to healthcare systems.

When a person is having a medical crisis, they generally do one of two things: go to the emergency room or call 911.

For homelessness, this is where we see the role of Coordinated Entry and the philosophy of "no wrong door."

If a person is in crisis and is about to become homeless, no matter where they contact the homeless service system, there should be the same, consistent triaging process to evaluate that person's needs and get them the help they need as quickly as possible.

From many years as a direct service provider, as well as through my current consulting work where I regularly host feedback sessions with people who are currently or have recently experienced homelessness, there are clear themes about what effective prevention requires.

- **A Clear and Simple Entry Point.** This should be a phone number that people can call or one, maybe two, major service providers where people know to go. The more entry points, the more confusion for the person in need.

- **The Entry Point (or Points) Should Be Well Advertised.** It should be posted at bus stops, in laundromats, and on community bulletin boards. It should be distributed to renters and landlords, given to students and parents at schools, and circulated among the local workforce. It should also be translated into different languages. Critically, people must be aware of this information before a crisis emerges.

- **The Entry Point Should Have Amazing Customer Service.** There should be a human being that is answering the phone number or welcoming people when they arrive at an in-person entry point. People in these jobs should provide exceptional customer experiences. When people in crisis are forced to leave voicemails or are treated disrespectfully during intake, they will understandably disengage.

- **The Customer Service Provider Should Be Armed with Resources.** When it comes to homelessness prevention, time is of the essence. An entry point should have immediate access to resources – typically short-term financial assistance and/or legal advocacy – that can be deployed within hours or days.

INSIGHT #10	Solving short-term homelessness requires both improving the systemic factors driving the cost of living <u>and</u> being able to prevent or rapidly rehouse people if they are facing homelessness.

E - Engage

If the homeless service system is not able to prevent a person from losing their housing, then that person, of course, ends up on the street.

It's at this point that we see the importance of having something like the "HOT Program" or a "by-name-list." In my experience, these are some of the most effective ways to identify, prioritize, and coordinate care for people who are currently experiencing homelessness.

Chapter 18 went into detail about how to manage these efforts, but there are a few additional systemic considerations worth highlighting here.

- **Data Sharing Is Critical** - Case conferencing efforts only work when partners are able to provide material updates on how clients are using and interacting with different services. Without effective data sharing agreements, it is impossible to dismantle organizational silos. (Importantly, people experiencing homelessness should not be denied access to care if they refuse to consent to data sharing agreements.)

- **Technology Should Facilitate Communication and Transparency** - The federal government requires that local communities receiving homelessness funding track client-level data and outcomes in a "Homelessness Management Information System" (HMIS). There are many different HMIS software systems, some of which make it easy to share data and coordinate care, while others are difficult to use and hinder effective collaboration.

- **Coordinated Outreach** - Outreach workers are social workers who work in the field to engage people experiencing unsheltered homelessness. In some communities, outreach can become a microcosm of the broader homeless industrial complex wherein different providers operate different outreach teams, none of whom are coordinated in who they are contacting or what they are helping clients work toward. Effective outreach looks like clear delineation across providers and subpopulations (e.g., people experiencing homelessness in different geographic regions, youth, veterans, families, people experiencing chronic homelessness).

Again, all of these efforts – data sharing, technological coordination, and outreach – should be "housing focused," meaning they are oriented toward moving people to housing placements as quickly as possible.

P - Place

Finally, there is the housing placement itself.

One of the most important roles of Coordinated Entry, like an emergency room, is to *rightsize* interventions.

If someone falls off a ladder while cleaning leaves from their gutter, the emergency room doesn't create a whole program about ladder safety prior to providing care. Instead, doctors provide the baseline level of required care (a cast, stitches, a cold compression) to help that person get back to living their life. Aside from a quick follow-up, the care relationship might end there.

Alternatively, if someone comes to the emergency room with life-threatening complications from diabetes, doctors would also immediately act to stabilize that person; however, since diabetes is a chronic health condition, doctors would likely refer this individual to another department to provide some level of ongoing care, either for a few months or even for the rest of that person's life.

When it comes to homelessness, housing placements can also vary by intensity and duration.

Fundamentally, the goal should be to help people resolve their housing crisis as quickly as possible while providing the minimal effective dose of ongoing supportive services to ensure housing retention.

Generally speaking, this boils down to three different approaches.

- **One-Time Financial Assistance** - Similar to homelessness prevention at the Triage step, many people experiencing homelessness simply need a one-time infusion of financial resources to get back inside. This might look like help with a security deposit for a new rental unit, or it could even look like facilitating a reconnection with friends or family (e.g., transportation assistance). To be clear, this is not giving a person money and asking them to leave the community. It is a targeted investment that will result in a person quickly regaining housing. Generally speaking, there is very little follow up needed after an intervention like this.

- **Rapid Rehousing** - For some people, especially individuals or families who have been outside for longer periods of time, Rapid Rehousing is short- to medium-term financial assistance (a few months to even a year or two) that is paired with supportive services. The idea is to get someone housed as quickly as possible and then provide ongoing assistance until that person or household can take over their own rent (e.g., gain regular employment) and/or coordinate their own care (e.g., effectively manage their behavioral health issues).

- **Permanent Supportive Housing** - If Housing First is the "how" for supporting the most vulnerable and at-risk people experiencing chronic homelessness, then permanent supportive housing is the "what." In most cases people experiencing chronic homelessness have significant ongoing needs and challenges, like the diabetic in our emergency room example, and it is unlikely that these highly vulnerable individuals are going to reach a point of complete self-sufficiency again (though that should always be the goal). To ensure long-term housing retention, permanent supportive housing pairs long-term rental subsidies with ongoing, wraparound case management support.

Emergency Shelter

In many communities, emergency shelter is also an important part of P - Placement.

At the most fundamental level, emergency shelter provides an alternative to having to sleep on the street, in a park, or in a vehicle.

Beyond ensuring this basic dignity, shelter capacity directly correlates with community impacts from homelessness.

For example, in California in 2019, at any given moment there was only emergency shelter capacity for approximately 28% of people experiencing homelessness.[1] In fact, that same year, over half of all people experiencing unsheltered homelessness in the United States resided in California.[2]

This lack of shelter is a huge factor behind the encampments and other humanitarian crises that have become a hallmark of homelessness on the West Coast.

Surprisingly though, shelter is not always an effective solution to homelessness.

In many communities, emergency shelter is often the physical embodiment of the "Natural Disaster" response to homelessness that we saw in Chapter 13. People are simply warehoused in these facilities and given an arbitrary time limit to "figure it out," similar to what victims of a fire, earthquake, or severe weather event might experience. Moreover, while they figure it out, they are often subjected to a litany of rules and regulations regarding increasing income, staying sober, and checking in and out at certain hours.

There will always be some people who thrive in this environment, but for people with more complex challenges, particularly people experiencing chronic homelessness, these settings very rarely lead to retention, let alone permanent housing placements.

In Marin County in 2017, when we were just beginning our systems change efforts, only 13% of people experiencing chronic homelessness were sheltered.[3] Thanks to Homeward Bound of Marin, Marin County's largest shelter provider, within two years, we were able to increase this utilization rate by nearly 200%.

When it comes to creating any shelter program (congregate shelters, non-congregate shelters, tiny home villages, sanctioned encampments, safe parking), the key continues to be remaining "housing focused."

To that end, shelter programs should ultimately be structured around the following outcomes:

1. The percentage of clients exiting to permanent housing. This number should be as high as possible.

2. The average length of stay (prior to a successful housing placement). This number should be as low as possible.

In other words, shelter should be a means to an end, not an end in itself.

Chapter 22:
Fixes That Fail

Before jumping into strategies for addressing the root causes of The Modern Homelessness Crisis, systems thinking offers one final warning about what it truly takes to solve entrenched, systemic problems.

> "Fixes that fail" occur when there is a problem, and a corrective action or fix seems to solve the issue; however, this action leads to some unforeseen consequences, [which forms] a feedback loop that either worsens the original problem or creates a related one.[1]

When it comes to homelessness, one of the clearest examples of "fixes that fail" is the idea of *universal* housing vouchers.

Housing Vouchers

Increasing rental housing prices are one of the biggest contributing factors to The Modern Homelessness Crisis.

Presently, one of our country's most significant rental housing supports is the "Housing Choice Voucher" (or as it's more commonly known, the Section 8 Voucher).

The Section 8 Voucher was designed as an alternative to public housing. Rather than people living in government built and operated units, Section 8 Vouchers allow people to rent "anywhere" in the community, and there is abundant evidence to suggest that "being able to live anywhere" helps families more effectively escape poverty.[2]

People often think Section 8 means free housing. It doesn't.

A Section 8 voucher means that the recipient pays 30% of their income toward rent, and the government pays the remaining balance up to market rate.

There are, however, upper limits to what HUD will pay for a unit. These are called "Fair Market Rent" rates. In practice, this means it is actually quite difficult for people to "live anywhere" since they are limited to rental units that are under the Fair Market Rent cap.

Instead, Section 8 rental opportunities are often limited to impoverished communities, and in many cases, voucher holders never find anywhere to live, which results in losing the voucher altogether.

For example, in Dallas in 2017, about 60% of the people who received vouchers were unable to use them.[3]

Unlike need-based safety net programs like Medicare, where if you meet the qualifications you get the resource, there are a limited number of housing vouchers that are allocated through Housing Authorities all across the country.

As of 2017, only 11% of "qualifying" low-income renter households (i.e., households paying more than 30% of their income on housing) actually received housing assistance like a voucher.[4]

Universal Housing Vouchers

For many people, housing vouchers truly are the proverbial "golden ticket." They are the only way an individual or family can afford housing.

Consider the rental market in Marin County, CA.

In 2019, the median rent was $2,096.[5] If someone were receiving disability payments, then they would have earned roughly $900 a month. Even if a person on disability had dedicated 100% of their income to housing, they still could not have afforded the median unit.

178

To address this challenge, in 2018, Vice President Kamala Harris – then Senator Harris of California – introduced the "Rent Relief Act." The bill was designed to give a tax credit to any renter who spent more than 30% of their income on housing costs, essentially creating universal housing vouchers in the form of tax refunds.

Even though the bill did not pass, in the ensuing years Democrats have continued to call for a significant expansion of housing vouchers.

Personally, I don't mind paying higher taxes to fund poverty alleviation programs like housing vouchers. Systems thinking, however, has forced me to reevaluate both the effectiveness and unintended consequences of policies like universal vouchers.

Specifically, people are struggling to pay their rent because of a lack of affordable rental units and stagnating wages. So what happens if, instead of fixing those underlying problems, we give a bunch of money to renters (and by extension, their landlords)?

The Mechanics of Inequality

In his book *Capital in the Twenty-First Century*, economist Thomas Picketty argues that there are two primary ways in which people grow wealthier:

1. When the economy grows, this should lead to higher wages for the average worker.[6]

2. People can grow their wealth from returns on capital.[7] Capital is a fancy way of saying things we own that produce an economic benefit. Stocks and real estate are good examples. As the prices of stocks and real estate go up, the people who own those assets become wealthier.

Picketty's research for *Capital in the Twenty-First Century* focused on the growth rates of these two paths to wealth creation. In other words, how quickly are wages growing versus returns on assets?

At the risk of oversimplifying a very detailed analysis, Picketty's research essentially confirms the well-known adage "it takes money to make money."[8] Over the last century, returns on capital have been growing at a faster rate than wages.

This has a huge impact on economic inequality, primarily because such a small number of people own the vast majority of capital in this country. As capital keeps appreciating for that minority while everyone else is dependent on wages, the wealth divide continues to grow.

Picketty's work focused on stock market returns, but the same dynamic is playing out with real estate.

As housing prices continue to rise, homeowners are getting wealthier while renters are simply facing larger monthly expenses.

The result is startling. The average homeowner now has a net worth of $195,400, which is 36 times larger than the average renter's net worth of $5,400.[9]

Success to the Successful

I am not opposed to people building wealth. In fact, I think building wealth is one of the best buffers against becoming homeless.

What bothers me, however, is when the process of building wealth is manipulated.

Imagine I own a parking lot in a blighted urban area. As the years go by, more and more people start moving back into the neighborhood. Other people start investing capital in new restaurants and shopping areas. Developers start erecting skyscrapers. The City government allocates new funding for public art, public transit, and community events.

In short, through no real effort on my part, the value of my property has increased substantially.

Again, there is nothing inherently wrong with this.

In finance, "returns" are meant to reflect risk. If I bought that parking lot 20 years ago in an undesirable part of town, I took a big risk. There was no guarantee that that property would increase in value.

This is similar to the stock market. No one really knows how a company is going to perform in the future, and we each have to balance how much we're willing to risk (how much money we invest) to receive a reward (a profitable company).

Sometimes, however, there can be a powerful systemic archetype lurking just beneath the surface – Success to the Successful.

Success to the Successful occurs when wins/benefits/achievements lead to a privileged opportunity to create more wins/benefits/achievements. Put another way, when winners get to create the rules of the game, the system can result in unfair competition and unhealthy concentrations of power, influence, and advantage.

At its core, Success to the Successful is essentially an out of control, reinforcing feedback loop, as demonstrated in the following examples:

- "Make It Take It" Basketball - Every time someone makes a shot, they get the ball again rather than giving the other person a chance to score.

- Lobbying - Corporations make a profit. They use their profit to lobby the government to create / get rid of regulations. The new regulatory environment results in more profit, which can pay for more lobbying.

- Legacy Admissions - Some educational institutions have historically carved out an admission preference for legacy students (i.e., students whose parents attended the same institution).

This same Success to the Successful cycle is happening with housing prices.

Chapter 7 showed that housing prices are not rising because we've run out of lumber, land, or don't know how to build vertically. Housing prices are going up, especially in urban areas, because the housing market has been heavily regulated to prevent new development. Zoning limits what and where communities can build. Lawsuits and other regulatory barriers prevent, slow, and stall the process even further.

Subsidizing Inequality

Rather than fixing these underlying issues, an idea like universal housing vouchers simply subsidizes a manipulated market's failure to create sufficient housing.

Importantly, these subsidies aren't floating out into the ether. They are real financial payments going to real people.

In his book *Evicted: Poverty and Profit in the American City*, Princeton Professor Matthew Desmond does an amazing job humanizing the rental housing crisis unfolding all across this country.

Interestingly, Desmond closes the book arguing for universal housing vouchers, even as he makes a telling observation about what's happening with another major poverty alleviation measure – the Earned Income Tax Credit (EITC), which is a federal tax refund for working people living in poverty.

Desmond, who had embedded himself with struggling renters, found that when people receive their EITC refund checks, many end up literally handing it over to their landlord to catch up on past-due rent.

> Today, if evictions are lowest each February, it is because many members of the city's working poor dedicate some or all of their Earned Income Tax Credit to pay back rent. In many cases, this annual benefit is as much a boost to landlords as to low-income working families.[10]

With this observation, we see a major potential pitfall of a policy like universal housing vouchers.

In the short run, yes, they would make rent more affordable. In the long run, however, by not solving the root issue driving increasing housing prices, they could exacerbate one of the major feedback loops driving economic inequality.

- Government policies have limited housing supplies.

- Limited supplies drive up the cost of housing.

- Rather than bringing down the cost of housing by increasing housing supplies, the government provides a subsidy to people paying too much money for housing.

- These subsidies are almost immediately transferred to property owners in the form of higher or past-due rent.

- Property owners can use this money to buy even more properties and/or lobby for more regulations, thus perpetuating the cycle.

As we'll see in the next chapter, housing vouchers are an important *part* of solving The Modern Homelessness Crisis, but they are not the whole solution.

Chapter 23:
The Big Eight

To truly solve homelessness in this country, we must begin to reverse the systemic conditions that are making it so much harder for people to be self-sufficient and/or get the help they need when they are struggling.

In Part 2, we looked at over 20 different factors driving The Modern Homelessness Crisis. I could have easily included 20 more, ranging from:

- The family and community ostracization and disconnection that disproportionately sends members of the LGBTQ community to the streets

- Young people who age out of the foster care system with nowhere to go

- The role of domestic violence and cycles of abuse within families

- The cost of healthcare and the fact that medical bills are the leading cause of bankruptcy in this country[1]

- The quality of schools and how that impacts future earning potential

While all of these issues deserve a solution, I want to leave you with what I consider to be the "Big Eight" policies and principles that, if enacted, would most significantly move the needle toward preventing homelessness in our country.

This chapter could easily be its own full section, even its own book, but for now, my hope is simply to spark a conversation about the type of systemic change our country so desperately needs.

#1: It's Possible

The ultimate solution to The Modern Homeless Crisis is simply believing it is possible.

According to systems theorist Daniel Kim,

> *Mental Models* are the beliefs and assumptions we hold about how the world works. We can view these assumptions as "systemic structure generators" ... *Vision* is our picture of what we want for our future. It is the guiding force that determines the mental models we hold as important as we pursue our goals.[2]

We saw the power of mental models in Chapter 19 with "Treatment First."

Many communities believe that people must first address the underlying reason(s) they became homeless before they can access permanent housing. The result is a jumbled web of different programs and services that seek to address the circumstances that led to someone becoming homeless without actually prioritizing ending their homelessness.

When it comes to homelessness overall, one of the most pervasive and defeating mental models is the notion that it is simply an unsolvable problem.

Sadly, this belief often becomes a self-fulfilling prophecy.

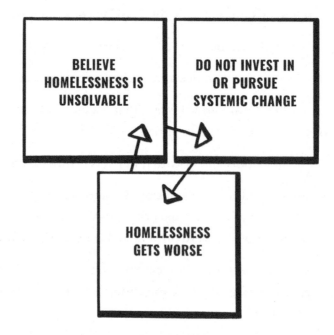

Rather than being a perpetual, unchanging phenomenon, there have been many eras of homelessness throughout our nation's history, each with its own unique socioeconomic causes.

The goal of this book has been to make these policies – and the way they interact – explicit, especially for The Modern Homelessness Crisis. By doing so, I hope it is easier to see that homelessness is not inevitable. Instead, it is the consequence of a specific portfolio of housing, economic, racial, and behavioral health policies.

If we believe in our hearts and minds that we can change these policies, then we *will* end homelessness in our country.

#2: National Service

For me, the belief that it is possible to end homelessness never would have happened if it weren't for national service.

I graduated from college in 2008. My plan at the time was to go to law school, so I moved back to my hometown of Richmond, VA, and started working at a local law firm to get a taste for the field while I studied for the LSAT (the entry exam for law school).

While I loved my co-workers, much to my surprise, I hated the job. My day-to-day workload consisted of thumbing through injured peoples' medical records to help find ways to defend insurance companies against accident claims.

Sadly, things in my personal life weren't much better. Having officially entered "the real world," I was finally grasping the true extent of my unhealthy relationship with alcohol.

I was depressed, anxious, and desperate for a change.

In an effort to salvage some meaning in my life and potentially find a new career path in the process, I started taking time off from work to volunteer in the community. I helped out at the local Holocaust Museum, "urban gardened" at the science museum, and even got an internship with the City of Richmond's Economic Development Department, but none of these opportunities truly resonated with me.

I was on the verge of giving up (being a lawyer must be better than being a paralegal, right?) when I stumbled on Project Homeless Connect (PHC).

Shortly after arriving at my first PHC event in the fall of 2009, I was connected with an elderly homeless woman named Mary. My assignment was to help her navigate the event space, which filled an entire exhibit hall at the Richmond Convention Center.

We connected with employers, free dental services, and a healthcare provider for people with HIV/AIDs (she was the first person I had ever met with HIV/AIDs). We had a great time together, but after about an hour, it felt like Mary hadn't really made *the* connection that was going to help her end her homelessness, so I turned to her and asked what I should have asked in the beginning: "What do *you* think you need?"

She leveled me with her quiet reply, "I just need help finding an apartment." I smiled at the simplicity of the request and told her we weren't going to find a landlord wandering around the convention center, so we went over to one of the event organizers and asked if we could leave to go look for apartments. I was hooked.

As I began to wonder whether there might be an opportunity to do this work for a living, I discovered AmeriCorps. Founded in 1965, AmeriCorps is the domestic version of the PeaceCorps, which is a federal program that coordinates long-term volunteer assignments in "difficult" parts of the world. There are a variety of AmeriCorps programs, and I gravitated toward VISTA.

With VISTA (which is more of a "capacity-building" role similar to the Peace-Corps), rather than being randomly assigned to a job, you actually apply for year-long positions. I was looking for assignments anywhere west of the Mississippi, and whether it was blind chance or a graceful nudge, I discovered that the City of San Jose was recruiting for the "Santa Clara County Project Homeless Connect Coordinator."

I had zero experience with event planning or community organizing, let alone homeless outreach, but I felt like this was too big of a coincidence to pass up. I pleaded my case and, somehow, got the job.

That opportunity completely changed the course of my life, so much so that I have often felt that if I wasn't working to end homelessness, I would want to commit myself to the cause of expanding opportunities for national service.

On some level, I truly believe the future of our country depends on a policy like this.

We are living through one of the most polarized and partisan periods in our country's history. We seek agreement with those who already agree with us and we are quick to dismiss differing perspectives. In our increasingly digital age, it's easy to lob insults and critiques through social media, but it's hard to bring people together, find ways to compromise, and drive tangible change in the real world.

For a highly complex problem like homelessness, which requires consensus-building across so many different stakeholders and points of view, it is absolutely essential that we learn to cultivate empathy and have the courage to work with people who we might not always agree with.

When I originally came to the Bay Area, I had no idea what to expect. I had spent my entire life in Virginia, and even though San Jose is the 10th largest city in the country, before I made the move, I couldn't point it out on a map. In fact, I initially thought it was in Southern California (and was pretty disappointed by how cold Bay Area summers are).

We all think our towns, our cities, or our neighborhoods are the center of the universe, but they're not. There are over 300 million people scattered across our vast and sprawling country, yet less than half of us have visited more than 10 states.[3]

I'll never forget pulling off the freeway into San Jose. There were signs in languages I had never seen before. There were people who looked very different from the people I grew up around. And if I'm really honest, I thought I made a huge mistake.

Gradually, however, I began making new friends. I started eating new foods and learning about different cultures. I experienced profound generosity, openness, and love from people with very different backgrounds, particularly the unhoused folks I was working with.

This experience gave me a radically new perspective, and hesitancy turned into profound gratitude.

I often wonder, what if every young person could have an experience like that?

I imagine young people from New York City going to the middle of Kansas or young people from Alabama and Mississippi volunteering on Skid Row in Los Angeles.

I then like to imagine what this country would be like 20, 30, even 50 years from now, when you could ask almost any other living American – *what did you do during your year of service?*

What would our civic discourse be like then? What would it feel like to be an American then?

I guarantee that we would think anything, including ending homelessness, was possible.

#3: Incorporating Lived Experience

While it's critical to get more people involved with this issue – advocating, building homes, becoming social workers – when it comes to homelessness and gaining a new perspective, it's extremely important to consider one of the most powerful points of view of all – people who are currently or who have previously been homeless.

One of the greatest barriers to systems change work is not including the voices of people who are actually involved in that system.

A few years ago, I stumbled on an incredible essay entitled "The Reductive Seduction of Other People's Problems," which explores what can happen when idealistic people begin dabbling in the lives of others. It begins with a powerful analogy:

> Let's pretend, for a moment, that you are a 22-year-old college student in Kampala, Uganda. You're sitting in class and discreetly scrolling through Facebook on your phone. You see that there has been another mass shooting in America, this time in a place called San Bernardino. You've never heard of it. You've never been to America. But you've certainly heard a lot about gun violence in the U.S. It seems like a new mass shooting happens every week.
>
> You wonder if you could go there and get stricter gun legislation passed. You'd be a hero to the American people, a problem-solver, a lifesaver. How hard could it be? Maybe there's a fellowship for high-minded people like you to go to America after college and train as social entrepreneurs. You could start the nonprofit organization that ends mass shootings, maybe even win a humanitarian award by the time you are 30.
>
> Sound hopelessly naïve? Maybe even a little deluded? It is. And yet, it's not much different from how too many Americans think about social change in the "Global South."
>
> If you asked a 22-year-old American about gun control in this country, she would probably tell you that it's a lot more complicated than taking some workshops on social entrepreneurship and starting a non-profit. She might tell her counterpart from Kampala about the intractable nature of our legislative branch, the long history of gun culture in this country and its passionate defenders, the complexity of mental illness and its treatment. She would perhaps mention the added complication of agitating for change as an outsider.
>
> But if you ask that same 22-year-old American about some of the most pressing problems in a place like Uganda — rural hunger or girl's secondary education or homophobia — she might see them as solvable. Maybe even easily solvable.[4]

As the article goes on to describe, there is nothing bad or wrong about trying to make the world a better place. That is natural and something we should encourage.

There is also nothing wrong with being a novice. How are people supposed to gain experience and expertise unless they have opportunities to get started?

Instead, problems arise when so-called "helpers" do not incorporate the feedback and expertise of the constituents they are trying to support.

There is an absolutely amazing organization called the Family Independence Initiative (FII) that has fully embraced this idea.

In his book *The Alternative: Most of What You Believe about Poverty Is Wrong*, FII's founder and MacArthur Genius Award winner, Mauricio Miller, describes our culture's pervasive belittling of people living in poverty. On one end of the political spectrum, people living in poverty are often seen as lazy, fraudulent, and/or undisciplined. On the other side, people living in poverty are often seen as helpless, needing extensive support from "professionals" who know how best to help.

In reality, poverty in the United States, like homelessness, is a relatively brief and short-term experience. As Miller has observed:

> We regularly hear that huge numbers of people are "stuck" in poverty, generally 14 to 18 percent of our population, but what did the [Census Bureau studies] find? Between 2005 and 2007 only 3% continued in poverty after those three years and between 2009 and 2012 only 2.7% continued living under the poverty line income.[5]

Miller contends that the overwhelming majority of people living in poverty know perfectly well how to take care of themselves. They simply lack sufficient financial resources to do so because of the systemic issues we've looked at in this book, such as the cost of housing and/or the lack of a living wage.

To that end, FII's goals are to:

- Raise money

- Give it directly to people in need

- Coordinate learning opportunities among the people receiving aid so they can share their wisdom in a peer setting

FII believes in this strategy so strongly that they have terminated staff members who have attempted to give advice to clients outside of these parameters.

Not every organization can or should operate like FII, especially for people with more complex needs and entrenched histories of poverty, trauma, or other behavioral health challenges. However, it is a powerful model that speaks to the fact that people living in poverty are resourceful, reflective, and wise, and our systems can be dramatically improved by incorporating their feedback.

#4: Deregulate Housing

As we learned in Part 2, and building off Miller's observation, for many Americans struggling with poverty or homelessness, the issue is simply a math problem – people do not have enough disposable income for the ever rising cost of living.

There are many factors driving up the cost of rent in this country, but in my view, the biggest is the overregulation of housing development. Nowhere is this clearer to see than in California.

According to a 2015 report from the State of California's Legislative Analyst's Office:

> Housing in California has long been more expensive than most of the rest of the country. Beginning in about 1970, however, the gap between California's home prices and those in the rest of the country started to widen. Between 1970 and 1980, California home prices went from 30 percent above U.S. levels to more than 80 percent higher. This trend has continued. Today, an average California home costs $440,000, about two–and–a–half times the average national home price ($180,000). Also, California's average monthly rent is about $1,240, 50 percent higher than the rest of the country ($840 per month).

> California is a desirable place to live. Yet not enough housing exists in the state's major coastal communities to accommodate all of the households that want to live there. In these areas, community resistance to housing, environmental policies, lack of fiscal incentives for local governments to approve housing, and limited land constrains new housing construction. A shortage of housing along California's coast means households wishing to live there compete for limited housing. This competition bids up home prices and rents. Some people who find

California's coast unaffordable turn instead to California's inland communities, causing prices there to rise as well.[6]

Unsurprisingly, California's coastal communities (LA, the Bay Area, San Diego) are also where we witness some of the largest and most sustained numbers of people experiencing homelessness in the entire country.

A 2016 report from McKinsey Consulting projected that California alone needs to create 3.5 million new homes.[7] That's a lot of houses. And with the average new affordable housing unit costing $425,000, unless California taxpayers want to shell out approximately $1.5 trillion to pay for the creation of 3.5 million new affordable housing units, then the state must incentivize the private market to create more housing.[8]

"Deregulating housing" can happen in two ways.

First, we have to "upzone" single family neighborhoods. Encouragingly, in 2021, California joined other cities, towns, and even states such as Oregon to eliminate single family zoning across the state.

Eliminating this kind of zoning does not mean suddenly building skyscrapers in the suburbs. Instead, upzoning single family neighborhoods means permitting land that used to only allow one housing unit to instead permit two, three, or even four units.

According to the UC Berkeley Terner Center for Housing Innovation, a policy like this would immediately create approximately 700,000 new market feasible units.[9]

Building on this step, communities must then allow for even denser housing in job rich urban areas and along major transit corridors. This could simply be "by-right," meaning like single-family zoning, these areas are simply upzoned, and the market can act from there.

Alternatively, given well-founded past concerns about private sector disregard for the environment and low-income people displaced by new development (particularly people of color), government agencies can provide local communities with planning grants for something called a specific plan.

Specific plans allow local communities to come together to pre-approve development patterns that jive with local priorities and preferences. Once adopted, specific plans prevent one-off community groups or advocates from coming in and blocking individual projects in these larger pre-approved areas.

One of the biggest costs of new development, which can either prevent construction all together or pass on high prices to future residents, is uncertainty. When projects are drawn out over months and years (or even decades), the cost to build keeps going up.

Specific plans significantly reduce that uncertainty while also ensuring stakeholder voices and concerns are incorporated.

#5: Direct Financial Payments

In the late 1960s, in an effort to push back on the bureaucratic growth of the "welfare state," President Richard Nixon began wondering whether the most straightforward solution to poverty was simply giving money directly to households that needed it.

To vet this idea, President Nixon marshaled the resources of the federal government to run a series of pilots. Economist Rutger Bregman has written extensively about Nixon's idea and the unexpected results it yielded:

> Tens of millions of dollars were budgeted to provide a basic income for more than 8,500 Americans in New Jersey, Pennsylvania, Iowa, North Carolina, Indiana, Seattle, and Denver in what were also the first-ever large-scale social experiments to distinguish experimental and control groups.[10]

A primary question arose for researchers: would people work significantly less if they receive a guaranteed income? As Bregman goes on to summarize:

> Reductions in working hours were limited across the board. "The 'laziness' contention is just not supported by our findings," the chief data analyst of the Denver experiment said. "There is not anywhere near the mass defection the prophets of doom predicted." The decline in paid work averaged 9% per family, and in every state it was mostly twentysomethings and women with young children who worked less ...
>
> The "declines in hours of paid work were undoubtedly compensated in part by

other useful activities, such as search for better jobs or work in the home," noted the Seattle experiment's concluding report. For example, one mother who had dropped out of high school worked less in order to earn a degree in psychology and get a job as a researcher. Another woman took acting classes; her husband began composing music. "We're now self-sufficient, income-earning artists," she told the researchers. Among youth included in the experiment, almost all the hours not spent on paid work went into more education. Among the New Jersey subjects, the rate of high school graduations rose 30%.[11]

On a personal note, having spent almost half my career in workforce development, I know some of the challenges posed by the current welfare system. I have worked with countless people who were dependent on disability or other payments, and for many, it took years of advocacy to finally secure this financial lifeline.

There is a popular myth that people on this type of aid do not want to volunteer, work, or in some way participate in the community, but I have found the exact opposite to be true. The issue is that for people on public benefits, if they do start working again, they can lose these precious income supports, so if the job does not work out, they are back in a desperate situation.

Guaranteed direct payments get around this. If people receive funding, regardless of needing to show a documented disability, there is much more security and flexibility for people to dip their toes back into the workforce.

While this might sound like more of a politically liberal idea, historically, this type of policy has enjoyed support from many prominent conservatives, ranging from presidential candidate and US Senator Mitt Romney to the iconic libertarian economist Milton Friedman (who called it a "negative income tax"). President Donald Trump even supported direct financial payments during the COVID-19 Pandemic.

Among conservatives, the idea of direct payments aligns with some of the critical insights from Mauricio Miller and FII.

Rather than creating a sprawling bureaucracy to administer various social service programs, the idea is that the vast majority of people know how to manage their own lives – they simply need more money.

Importantly, as I cautioned in the last chapter, a policy like this must be paired with structural reforms to the cost of living (e.g., bringing down the cost of rent), as well as economic inequality more generally (e.g., a more progressive tax code that prevents runaway capital accumulation).

#6: Reparations for Black Americans

Shortly after the Japanese attack on Pearl Harbor during World War II, the US government, under direction from President Franklin D. Roosevelt, forcibly relocated approximately 120,000 Japanese Americans to internment camps (including 30,000 children), citing fears of collusion with the Japanese government.

Beyond the trauma of living in these internment camps, the people and families that were forced to these areas suffered significant material and financial losses.

- Internees could only bring the personal property they could carry to the camps, thus being forced to leave behind irreplaceable personal items.

- Business owners were forced to close down their stores and forfeit those income streams.

- The overwhelming majority of internees came from California, Oregon, and Washington, and these states banned the ownership of pre-war homes and farms, many of which had been building value for decades.

Amazingly, recognizing the horror and impact of this chapter in American history, the federal government actually took action to make amends for what happened.

In 1983, the Commission on Wartime Relocation and Internment of Civilians's report, *Personal Justice Denied*, found little evidence of Japanese disloyalty at the time and concluded that the incarceration had been the product of racism. As a result, it recommended that the government pay reparations to the internees.

In 1988, President Ronald Reagan signed into law the Civil Liberties Act of 1988, which officially apologized for the internment on behalf of the U.S. government and authorized a payment of $20,000 (equivalent to $44,000 in 2020) to each former internee who was still alive when the act was passed.

Reparations are compensation for a harm.

As we learned in Chapter 9, it is not an accident that in 2020, the average Black household had 1/10 the wealth of the average white household.[12] Indeed, this economic disparity helps to explain the 400%+ overrepresentation of Black Americans among people experiencing homelessness.[13]

Just like the material losses to Japanese Americans during World War II, we can catalog centuries of government-enabled financial abuse toward Black Americans:

- 250 years of slavery that barred Black Americans from the fruits of their labor

- State-sponsored violence against Black Americans during Jim Crow, leading to the murder of Black lives and the destruction of Black property

- Wage discrimination during the New Deal

- Destruction of Black neighborhoods during "slum clearance" programs

- Zoning black neighborhoods near factories and other public health threats, leading to lifelong disabilities

- Housing discrimination and redlining

Reparations would begin to right these wrongs.

#7: 1,000,000 Permanent Supportive Housing Units

Homelessness isn't just about economics. It's also about people's physical and mental well-being.

When I first started working for the City of San Rafael, one of my early tasks was to resolve the homelessness for a person who was essentially living in the lobby of City Hall. To the mayor, councilmembers, and City staff, this person had become emblematic of the system's inability to help a clearly vulnerable person.

As I would come to learn from working with this person, they were not lacking for financial resources. They grew up in one of the wealthiest enclaves of Marin County, and there were still family members in their life who were willing to step in to help.

Instead, two major barriers stood in their way:

1. This person could not live independently without intensive support. The last time they had been housed independently without support, they had gouged holes in the wall of their apartment, fearing surveillance equipment was tracking their movement.

2. While this person had moments of clarity about their mental health challenges, more often than not they lacked insight and actively denied having any problems.

According to the National Alliance on Mental Illness:

> When someone rejects a diagnosis of mental illness, it's tempting to say that [they're] 'in denial.' But someone with acute mental illness may not be thinking clearly enough to consciously choose denial. They may instead be experiencing "lack of insight" or "lack of awareness." The formal medical term for this medical condition is anosognosia, from the Greek meaning 'to not know a disease.'"[14]

These challenges require fundamentally different solutions than what we have looked at so far.

First, on the independent housing front, it is critical to remember the powerful link between deinstitutionalization and the rise of street homelessness among the severely mentally ill.

When policymakers originally proposed deinstitutionalization, they called for the creation of a robust network of community-based mental health treatment options, but that vision was never fully funded or realized.

Interestingly, having now directly witnessed hundreds of extremely vulnerable people who had been suffering from physical illness, traumatic brain injuries, substance abuse disorders, and significant mental illness challenges find long-term, find lasting success in Housing First programs (not to mention all of the national studies further corroborating the power of this intervention), I've come to a pretty simple conclusion – Housing First *is* the community-based mental health treatment that was envisioned so many decades ago.

This, in my view, is where housing vouchers are incredibly important.

For people with these long-term, life-altering diagnoses, yes, supportive housing providers are always working to reintegrate people in the community by way of new volunteer opportunities, social networks, and/or paid employment. However, for this particular subpopulation, I don't think that should be the expectation.

Instead, as a nation, we simply need to acknowledge that we need some level of ongoing permanent supportive housing for the most vulnerable among us, and we can do this by:

- Providing dedicated housing vouchers for people who have experienced chronic homelessness

- Ensuring the availability of intensive, wraparound services (in line with Housing First) once they are inside

How many permanent supportive housing units do we need to create? To make it simple, we should aim to replace at least the 1,000,000 Single Room Occupancy units that our country lost in the 1960s, 70s, and 80s.

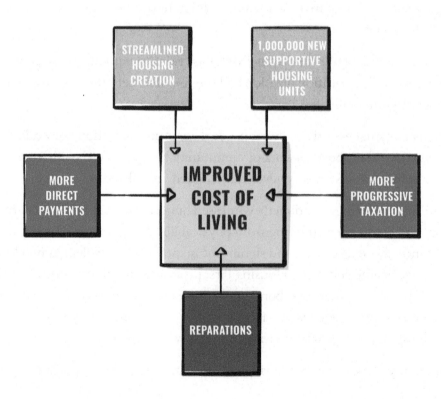

#8: Jury Trials for Compelling Treatment

Now, especially among the most progressive parts of the country, comes the really hard part.

Even with the expanded opportunities for Housing First, we have to acknowledge that there are still going to be an even smaller minority of people who have an extremely hard time accessing the support they need, and for these folks, we are going to have to revisit compelling treatment.

In my experience, even for people who are deeply in the grips of anosognosia, patience and perseverance can pay off.

In the case of the person living at San Rafael's City Hall, it took close to a year of near daily engagement efforts to:

1. Build sufficient trust

2. Catch this person at moments when they did have more insight so we could take baby steps toward housing.

If you want to find some of the most skilled and incredible mental health professionals in this country, look no further than the men and women providing street outreach to people with severe behavioral health issues.

Again and again, with enough time (three months, six months, a year), I have seen outreach workers build enough trust and partnership that even the most difficult cases become open to coming back inside.

In my experience, these success stories are the norm, rather than the exception, but we cannot ignore the exceptions.

Sadly, because of a variety of different factors, people can pass beyond the point of being responsive to outreach. Whether it's meth-induced psychosis on top of underlying mental health issues, "wet brain" (i.e., alcohol-induced dementia), or traumatic brain injury, *some* people become so impaired (they sustain so much structural damage to the brain) that it's almost impossible for them to have insight about their condition.[15]

As we observed in Chapter 10, at the beginning of the 20th Century, there was significant abuse in the "commitment" or "conservatorship" process.

As just one example, sexism was rife. Husbands, for example, would collude with doctors to have their wives locked up in mental health hospitals for "being crazy."

I never could have expected this, but as of finishing this chapter in the summer of 2021, pop singer Brittany Spears, who is currently challenging a conservatorship managed by her father, is yet again bringing public awareness to this process.

For all of the intense feelings around something as coercive as involuntary treatment or commitment, as Steven Seager describes in his book *Street Crazy*, there is actually a very old solution that could be used to further reform this process – the jury trial.

Rather than giving undue power to any one entity, like a doctor (who is narrowly focused on medical needs) or a judge (who is narrowly focused on the letter of the law), if conservatorship cases shifted to jury trials, it could help create a much more nuanced portrait of a person's life. For example, doctors and lawyers could testify, as could parents or other community service providers who might have a much longer and more detailed history of what this person has been experiencing.

If communities do not have sufficient outreach capacity as well as sufficient permanent supportive housing openings to try to proactively engage the most vulnerable people, I think it's hard to justify compelling treatment. However, assuming these conditions are met, some small percentage of people are still going to struggle significantly, and there are mechanisms like jury trials that could bring more humanity and holistic thinking to the situation.

It might seem inhumane to force someone into treatment, but is it any better to watch them slowly die in public, as we collectively walk by doing nothing?

We know how to solve The Modern Homelessness Crisis, and failing to act is a moral failure of the highest order:

> Neighbors in the Castro [a neighborhood in San Francisco] knew her as Princess Leia because she often wore her long hair in two buns on the sides of her head, sometimes held together with syringes. Supervisor Rafael Mandelman knew her as Individual M, a reference to her placement on his list of 17 distressed and

distressing people in his district whom he tries to help with intensive services. Countless others recognized her only as the woman they saw repeatedly walk into traffic at Castro and Market streets and narrowly miss getting whacked by a car. She prompted numerous calls to 911 and 311. But the concern could not save her. Not in this city long on professed compassion, but short on the help needed to make a difference. And so in an unsurprising end to her sad life, Mary Elaine Botts died Nov. 18 of a drug overdose. She was 28.[16]

Epilogue:
Homelessness in 2040

I began writing this book in the summer of 2017, and it took me nearly five years to finish.

With each passing year, I kept thinking a book like this wouldn't be needed.

Certainly, I kept hoping, our country was about to round a corner toward taking this issue seriously, toward making critical and long overdue investments, and toward measurably reducing homelessness once and for all.

Sadly, that did not happen.

Homelessness has continued to get worse in the United States, particularly in its largest metropolitan areas, and my hope is that this book can provide a much needed roadmap for community members, advocates, funders, civic leaders, and community-based organizations that are trying to drive meaningful change.

Homelessness is very simple.

People lack housing and we need to get them back inside.

Homelessness is also very complex.

The likelihood that a personal crisis will push someone to the streets is dependent on a complicated and interconnected web of socioeconomic systems - the rental housing market, the labor market, patterns of systemic racism, access to behavioral healthcare. Once someone is actually unhoused, there is then an equally complex maze of different programs, services, and community responses that can make it even harder for people to get back inside.

After 10+ years of trying to figure out how to navigate these systems, my goal with this book has been to concisely share the a-ha moments that helped me better understand what it will take to end homelessness in our country.

Reasons for Hope

I still deeply believe there is reason to hope.

In the San Francisco Bay Area, a new regional coalition across the nine Bay Area counties is forming, and it is committed to dramatically reducing unsheltered homelessness over the next three years while also tackling the upstream issues causing homelessness in the first place.

Public-private coalitions like this are emerging all across the country, including more communities joining the national Built for Zero movement.

At a state level in California, an unprecedented amount of money is being directed toward the acquisition of new housing and the creation of new services. There are also finally pushes to reform zoning and other land-use barriers to new housing.

As a result of the economic fallout from the COVID-19 pandemic, there seems to be more awareness that the economic divide in this country is continuing to grow, and working class people are struggling more than ever to keep up. The federal government has even experimented with nationwide direct financial payments.

The pandemic has also revealed the critical role of behavioral health as rates of mental illness and addiction have continued to climb.

Finally, increasing public awareness about disproportionate law enforcement responses in the Black community is leading to more momentum to reform historic patterns of systemic racism.

INSIGHT #1	Homelessness is best understood as a flow. It is a dynamic experience that people enter and exit.
INSIGHT #2	When seen as a flow, we observe that for the vast majority of people who become homeless, it is a one-time, brief experience lasting a few short weeks or months.
INSIGHT #3	While a crisis (e.g., a job loss, rent increase, relationship breakdown, health crisis) might catalyze an episode of homelessness, the likelihood of becoming homeless is ultimately the result of a complex interplay of other life circumstances - the broader economy, health conditions, family dynamics, neighborhood, social network.
INSIGHT #4	We are living through a distinct period of homelessness that began in the early 1980s, which I refer to as The Modern Homelessness Crisis.
INSIGHT #5	The Modern Homelessness Crisis is the result of multiple socioeconomic trends that are making it more likely for personal crises to push people into homelessness.
INSIGHT #6	In response to The Modern Homelessness Crisis, many communities have created well-intentioned but uncoordinated homeless service systems whose structural inefficiencies can perpetuate the very problems they are intended to solve.
INSIGHT #7	Moreover, many local communities often perceive it to be in their selfish, short-term interest to do as little as possible to solve homelessness, which ends up hurting everyone in the long-term.
INSIGHT #8	Effectively addressing The Modern Homelessness Crisis requires addressing two different problems: providing short-term assistance for people experiencing financial shocks and providing long-term care for people suffering from disabling health conditions.
INSIGHT #9	Housing First is the answer for providing long-term care for people who are suffering disabling health conditions and experiencing chronic homelessness.
INSIGHT #10	Solving short-term homelessness requires both improving the systemic factors driving the cost of living and being able to prevent / rapidly rehouse people if they are facing homelessness.

As the parent of two small children, all of this momentum makes me hopeful that The Modern Homelessness Crisis will be nothing more than a shameful chapter in their history books.

At the same time, the more I have immersed myself in systems thinking, the more it seems like the signs of our nation's next era of homelessness are already appearing.

Whether it's wildfires destroying homes on the West Coast, rising seas swallowing homes along the Atlantic and Gulf of Mexico, or more severe heat waves and droughts in the Southwest, unless we're able to do more to prevent the impending impacts of the climate crisis, millions of Americans could yet again find themselves on the road, trying to find somewhere to call home.

As much as this book has been about homelessness, it has also been about systems thinking.

My hope is that from climate change to immigration to sustainable supply chains, you can apply this set of tools to tackle the complex problem space(s) that you are most concerned about.

And with that, I leave you where we began:

> Hunger, poverty, environmental degradation, economic instability, unemployment, chronic disease, drug addiction, and war … persist in spite of the analytical ability and technical brilliance that have been directed toward eradicating them … because they are intrinsically systems problems – undesirable behaviors characteristic of the system structures that produce them. They will yield only as we reclaim our intuition, stop casting blame, see the system as the source of its own problems and find the courage and wisdom to restructure it.[1]

Stay Involved

As a complement to this book, I will be providing additional information, updates, research, tools, and training opportunities at:

www.howtosolvehomelessness.org.

Acknowledgments

In the summer of 2010, I threw everything I owned into the trunk of my car and drove across the country to start a new life in California.

Those first few years were extremely difficult, and I came incredibly close to throwing in the towel. In hindsight, however, I can't imagine my life having turned out any other way.

When I reflect on what it took to continue on, let alone get to a point that I could write a whole book about the experience, it all comes down to the people.

I will never be able to thank everyone who impacted this journey, but here's my best attempt.

First and foremost, I have to thank the three people who took a chance on me and gave me my most significant career opportunities: Kelly, Eileen, and Jim. You forever changed the course of my life.

From there, every step of the way has involved being part of amazing teams.

It all started with VISTA: Katie, Danny, and Ben.

Then there was DST: Chad, Logan, Brandon, Jaclyn, Greg, Chris, Kelty, Angelique, Alena, Maureen, Zia, Isa, Jimmy, Cliff, Elfreda, Tashia, Julia, Michelle, and Marianna.

Then came the City: Lynn, Cristine, Danielle, Kate, Rachel, Gary, Andrew, Rafat, Catherine, Sean, Susan, Nadine, Chief Gray, Chief White, Chief Sinnot, Chief Bishop, Nadine, Lindsay, Brenna, Ana, Steve M, Steve S, Scott, Carl, Roy,

Glenn, Dave, Ali, Laraine, Lisa, Rob, Bill, Ryan, Omar, Doris, Vinh, Jessica, Henry, Debbie, Van, Ethan, Raffi, Quinn, Cory, Christine, Paul, Jinder, Michelle, Lidia, Becky, Margaret, Rhonda, Shibani, Zak, Todd, Larry, DJ, Luis, Sylvia, Jennifer, Erin, Dylan, Crystal, Thomas, Kyle, and Matt. At one point early on we did a survey that found that 54% of City employees were in some way impacted by homelessness in their jobs, so I know the team was even bigger.

Through my role with the City and eventually Opening Doors Marin, there were all of the friendships and partnerships through MASH: Howard, Christine, Heather, Ashley, Carrie, Ken, Charis, Gary, Paul, Mary Kay, Anna, LaSaunda, Colin, Connie, Katy, Cayenne, Nikolas, Kimberly, Lewis, Tammy, Mark, Linda, Cia, Simon, Cheryl, Karen, Jesse, and Zoe.

There have also been so many other amazing friends, mentors, and community partners that have impacted this journey: Sara, the Berkeley Haas family, Sheri, Joanne, Jules, Carol, Paula, Cecilia, Lorenzo, Katie, Damon, Kirsten and ELGL, the CivicMakers crew, Eric, Adam, Dr. Derek Van Dangle, Dominique, Daniel, Marie, Nancy, Zak, Stacey, Alan, Johnathan, Wayne, Amy, Omar, Leelee, James, Pat, Meredith, Scott, Ellen, Nick, Lisel, Jan, Philip, Consuelo, Michael, and Dana.

And of course, there have been all of the absolutely incredible people with lived experience of homelessness who allowed me to be a part of their lives, particularly: JB, Connie, Eugene, Dennis, Mark P, Malfred, Tom, Jovan, James, Annie, Francois, Dallas, Brooke, Alexis, Pierre, Bailey, Michael D, Michael J, Robert, Mark C, Maureen, Rodney, Denise, Shannon, Leif, Andre, Anita, Kevin, Judy, Paul, Lovely, Letitia, Gary, Leo, Peter, Will, Holly, Kenny, Warren, Nelson, Regina, Azim, Michaelangelo, Andre, Pam, and Griff.

This book never would have happened without Rebecca. Thank you, thank you, thank you for being there for me the last five years. I am so extremely grateful for your editorial brilliance.

And to Jen and Michaela, I could not have gotten this project across the finish line without your support.

Finally, to the ladies in my life - Joanne, Lucy, Eleanor - I love you so much.

Appendix

Appendix

A Technical Note on Systems Mapping

As noted at the end of Chapter 7, given that this book is intended for a general reader with no previous systems thinking or homelessness experience, I decided to deviate from traditional systems diagramming techniques in the hope of making my systems maps as clear and understandable as possible.

I do, however, want to provide you with a more accurate description of the systems mapping process.

You have already seen the first two steps:

1. Create "nodes" for each element in the system.

2. Use arrows between the nodes to denote the directional flow of interconnections.

In the maps in the book, I then used descriptions in the nodes to describe what was happening. For example, in Chapter 7, I said "the elimination of 1,000,000 SRO units" leads to "constrained housing supply = higher prices."

Technically, this is incorrect. Instead:

3. When creating nodes, the verbiage should simply be a stock (i.e., things, stuff, activities, actions, etc. that can be quantified).

4. Nodes should not include descriptions or adjectives describing the

stock. Nodes should also not include verbiage that reaches some sort of conclusion.

Using the SRO example, a more accurate systems map would have a node called "SRO Units" with an arrow pointing to "Total Housing Units" with another arrow then pointing to "Housing Prices."

5. Finally, the arrows between nodes should include either a "+" or a "-" to denote casual and/or correlated relationships. More specifically, a "+" means the two nodes move together (i.e., if one goes up, the other goes up; if one goes down, the other goes down). A "-" means the two nodes move in opposite directions (i.e., as one node goes up, the other goes down).

Based on the logic laid out in Chapter 7, the first arrow between "Supply of SRO Units" and "Total Housing Units" would have a "+" sign (i.e., as the supply of SRO Units goes down, the Total Housing Units also go down), and the arrow between "Total Housing Units" and "Housing Prices" would have a "-" sign (i.e., as the number of Total Housing Units goes down, Housing Prices would go up).

To visualize the difference, I am including an accurate systems map of the housing dynamics leading to homelessness:

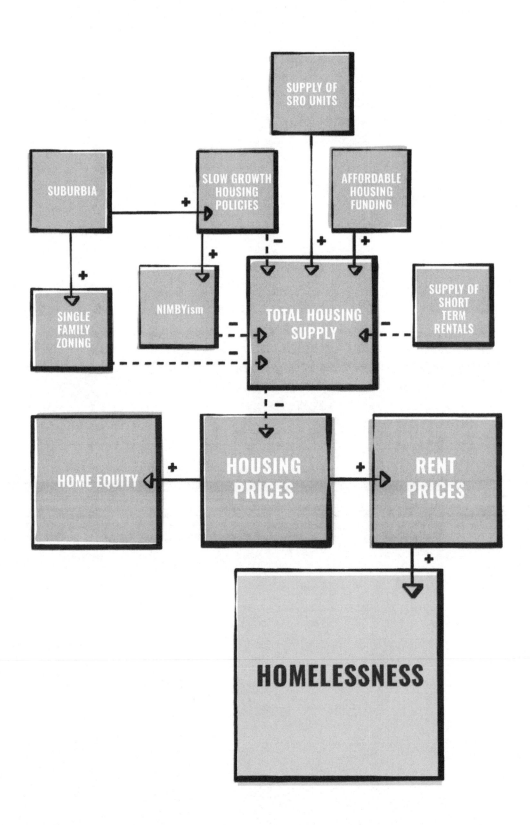

Notes and Illustration Sources

Please note that all illustrations, graphics, and tables, as well as some photographs, are the custom and copyrighted materials of Andrew Hening (hereinafter, the "Author") and cannot be copied or reproduced without the Author's consent. Licensed photographs and custom illustrations based on data sources not cited in the text itself are identified below.

Chapter 1: A New Way of Seeing

1. Andrew Hening, "Marin Voice: San Rafael's streets team project shows homeless just need a chance," *Marin Independent Journal*, last modified August 6, 2014, https://www.marinij.com/2014/08/06/marin-voice-san-rafaels-streets-team-project-shows-homeless-just-need-a-chance/.

2. Donella H. Meadows, *Thinking in Systems* (Hartford: Chelsea Green Publishing, 2008), 4.

3. *Bay Area Homelessness: A Regional View of a Regional Crisis*, Bay Area Council Economic Institute, April 2019, p. 6, http://www.bayareaeconomy.org/files/pdf/Homelessness_Report_2019_web.pdf.

4. M. Jaross, Y. Kwak, & J. Gallant, *Marin County Homeless Count and Survey Comprehensive Report 2019, Applied Survey Research*, p. 16, https://www.marinhhs.org/sites/default/files/files/servicepages/2019_07/2019hirdreport_marincounty_final.pdf.

Chapter 2: Systems Thinking

1. Donella H. Meadows, *Thinking in Systems*, 2.

2. Ibid., 17-18.

3. Ibid., 25.

Chapter 3 - 37 Days

1. "Category 1: Literal Homelessness," HUD Exchange, https://www.hudexchange.info/homelessness-assistance/coc-esg-virtual-binders/coc-esg-homeless-eligibility/four-categories/category-1/.

2. M. Jaross, Y. Kwak, & J. Gallant, *Marin County Homeless Count and Survey Comprehensive Report 2019*.

3. Ibid.

4. Ibid.

5. Ibid.

6. Ibid.

7. Ibid.

8. Ibid.

9. K. Hopper, M. Shinn, E. Laska, M. Meisner, and J. Wanderling, "Estimating Numbers of Unsheltered Homeless People Through Plant-Capture and Postcount Survey Methods," *American Journal of Public Health* 98, no. 8 (2008): 1438–1442.

10. "Don't Count on It: How the HUD Point-in-Time Count Underestimates the Homelessness Crisis in America," National Law Center on Homelessness & Poverty, 2017, p. 12, https://homelesslaw.org/wp-content/uploads/2018/10/HUD-PIT-report2017.pdf.

11. "Appendix B - Background Report," *City of San Rafael 2015 – 2023 Housing Element*, City of San Rafael, California, January 5, 2015, pp. B1-2, https://storage.googleapis.com/proudcity/sanrafaelca/uploads/19.-GP-2020-Appendix-B-Housing-Bkgrnd_Reprint-04.28.17-FINAL2.pdf.

12. *Marin County Homeless Census & Survey Comprehensive Report 2017*, Applied Survey Research, p.14, https://www.marinhhs.org/sites/default/files/files/servicepages/2017_07/pit-report-marincounty-final.pdf.

13. M. H. Morton, A. Dworsky, & G. M. Samuels, *Missed Opportunities: Youth Homelessness in America - National Estimates*, Chapin Hall at the University of Chicago, 2017, https://voicesofyouthcount.org/wp-content/uploads/2017/11/VoYC-National-Estimates-Brief-Chapin-Hall-2017.pdf.

14. "Part 1: Point-in-Time Estimates of Homelessness," *The 2016 Annual Homeless Assessment Report (AHAR) to Congress*, The U.S. Department of Housing and Urban Development, November 2016, https://www.nhipdata.org/local/upload/file/2016-AHAR-Part-%20reduced(1).pdf.

15. Ibid.

16. John M. Quigley, Steven Raphael, and Eugene Smolensky, "Homeless in America, Homeless in California," *The Review of Economics and Statistics* 83, no. 1 (2001), p. 38, https://urbanpolicy.berkeley.edu/pdf/QRS_REStat01PB.pdf.

17. Daniel Flaming, "Home Not Found: The Cost of Homelessness in Silicon Valley," Economic Roundtable, last modified May 26, 2015, https://economicrt.org/press-release/2349/.

18. Ibid.

Chapter 4: What Would You Do?

1. *Bay Area Homelessness: A Regional View of a Regional Crisis*, 6.

2. Bridget Deschenes, *"10 Things to Keep in Mind if You Are Serious About Ending Homelessness,"* OrgCode, https://www.orgcode.com/blog/10-things-to-keep-in-mind-if-you-are-serious-about-ending-homelessness.

3. Author's recollection from a presentation by Iain De Jong in 2017, Santa Rosa, CA.

4. Ibid.

5. "Part 1: Point-in-Time Estimates of Homelessness," *The 2019 Annual Homeless Assessment Report (AHAR) to Congress*, The U.S. Department of Housing and Urban Development, January 2020, p. 12, https://www.huduser.gov/portal/sites/default/files/pdf/2019-AHAR-Part-1.pdf.

6. *Marin County Homeless Census & Survey Comprehensive Report 2019, Applied Survey Research*, p. 45, https://www.marinhhs.org/sites/default/files/files/service-pages/2019_07/2019hirdreport_marincounty_final.pdf.

7. *Behavioral Health Barometer: California, Volume 5: Indicators as measured through the 2017 National Survey on Drug Use and Health and the National Survey of Substance Abuse Treatment Services*, Substance Abuse and Mental Health Services Administration, 2019, pp. 25-26, https://store.samhsa.gov/sites/default/files/d7/priv/california-bh-barometervolume5-sma19-baro-17-us.pdf.

8. "Facts and Statistics," National Alliance on Mental Illness - California, https://namica.org/what-is-mental-illness/facts-statistics/, and *Behavioral Health Barometer: California*, Volume 5, 32.

9. Till von Wachter, Marianne Bertrand, Harold Pollack, Janey Rountree, and Brian Blackwell, *Predicting and Preventing Homelessness in Los Angeles*, California Policy Lab, September 2019, https://www.capolicylab.org/wp-content/uploads/2019/12/Predicting_and_Preventing_Homelessness_in_Los_Angeles.pdf.

10. Daniel Wilco, "How the new 3-point line might affect college basketball," NCAA, last modified November 8, 2019, https://www.ncaa.com/news/basketball-men/article/2019-10-03/how-new-3-point-line-might-affect-college-basketball#:~:text=College%20basketball%27s%203%2Dpoint%20line,distance%20used%20in%20international%20basketball.

Chapter 5 - 1982 (12)

1. Nancy Isenberg, *White Trash: The 400-Year Untold History of Class in America* (New York: Viking Press, 2016), 10.

2. Ibid., 25.

3. Ibid., 85.

4. Derick Moore, "Fun Facts: From Counties Named Liberty to $368.6M Worth of Fireworks Sold," United States Census Bureau, last modified July 2, 2019, https://www.census.gov/library/stories/2019/07/july-fourth-celebrating-243-years-of-independence.html, and "Africans in British North America," monticello.org, https://www.monticello.org/slavery/paradox-of-liberty/african-slavery-in-colonial-british-north-america/africans-in-british-north-america/.

5. Aaron Lake Smith, "Death of the American Hobo," VICE, last modified November 10, 2012, https://www.vice.com/da/article/4wq9dq/death-of-the-american-hobo-0012987-v19n10.

6. Layal Shafee, "What Tramps Cost Nation," *The New York Telegraph*, 1911.

7. Aaron Lake Smith, "Death of the American Hobo."

8. Kimberly Amadeo, "9 Principal Effects of the Great Depression," The Balance, last modified January 27, 2022, https://www.thebalance.com/effects-of-the-great-depression-4049299#:~:text=The%20Great%20Depression%20of%201929,and%20deflation%20soared%20above%2010%25, and David C. Wheelock, "Changing the Rules: State Mortgage Foreclosure Moratoria During the Great Depression," *The Federal Reserve Bank of St. Louis Review* (November/December 2008), https://files.stlouisfed.org/files/htdocs/publications/review/08/11/Wheelock.pdf.

9. Stephen Talbot, "'To Have and Have Not': The Early Days of Bay Area Homelessness," KQED, last modified June 27, 2016, https://www.kqed.org/news/10997967/to-have-and-have-not-a-look-back-at-the-early-days-of-the-bay-areas-homeless-problem.

Illustrations

1. *Unemployed Men Hop Train*, 1933, https://commons.wikimedia.org/wiki/File:UnemployedMenHopTrain.jpg.

2. *Hooverville on the Seattle tideflats*, 1933, 1933, https://commons.wikimedia.org/wiki/File:Hooverville_on_the_Seattle_tideflats,_1933_(50495168952).jpg.

3. *Francine Orr, A Homeless Woman in Los Angeles*, Licensed Photograph – 07138207, *Los Angeles Times*, Polaris.

Chapter 6: Mapping a Complex System

1. *What America Believes About Homelessness*, Invisible People,

December 2020, https://invisiblepeople.tv/2020research/ What_America_Believes_About_Homelessness_IP.pdf.

2. Donella Meadows, *Thinking in Systems*, 3.

Chapter 7 - Housing

1. *The State of the Nation's Housing 2020, Joint Center for Housing Studies of Harvard University, 2020*, p. 34, https://www.jchs.harvard.edu/sites/default/files/ reports/files/Harvard_JCHS_The_State_of_the_Nations_Housing_2020_Report_ Revised_120720.pdf.

2. Ibid.

3. Howard Schwartz, *"Fuel Implications of Suburb-To-Suburb Commuting," The Fuse,* last modified January 29, 2018, http://energyfuse.org/ fuel-implications-of-suburb-to-suburb-commuting/.

4. Richard Rothstein, *The Color of Law: A Forgotten History of How Our Government Segregated America* (New York: Liveright, 2017), 63.

5. Richard Rothstein, *The Color of Law*, 70, and "75 Years of the GI Bill: How Transformative It's Been," U.S. Department of Defense, last modified January 9, 2019, https://www.defense.gov/News/Feature-Stories/story/ Article/1727086/75-years-of-the-gi-bill-how-transformative-its-been/.

6. Ibid.

7. Kenneth T. Jackson, *Crabgrass Frontier: The Suburbanization of the United States* (New York: Oxford University Press, 1987), 206, 235.

8. Ibid.

9. "Levitt & Sons, Inc. v. DIV. AGAINST DISCRIMINATION, ETC.," Justia US Law, https://law.justia.com/cases/new-jersey/supreme-court/1960/31-n-j-514-0.html.

10. "What did it cost?" in "Interstate Frequently Asked Questions," U.S. Department of Transportation Federal Highway Administration, https://www.fhwa.dot.gov/ interstate/faq.cfm#question7.

11. "San Jose Housing Market," Redfin, https://www.redfin.com/city/17420/CA/ San-Jose/housing-market.

12. Emily Badger and Quoctrung Bui, "Cities Start to Question an American Ideal: A House With a Yard on Every Lot," *The New York Times,* last modified June 18, 2019, https://www.nytimes.com/interactive/2019/06/18/upshot/cities-across-america-question-single-family-zoning.html.

13. Ibid.

14. Ibid.

15. Ibid.

16. Ibid.

17. Paul Rogers, "Bay Area open space: 75 percent is being protected, but 300,000 acres are still at risk," *The Mercury News*, last modified May 22, 2012, https://www.mercurynews.com/2012/05/22/bay-area-open-space-75-percent-is-being-protected-but-300000-acres-are-still-at-risk/#:~:text=Roughly%2075%20percent%20of%20all,farming%20or%20other%20rural%20uses.

18. "Marin Housing Market," Redfin, https://www.redfin.com/county/323/CA/Marin-County/housing-market.

19. "Linking CEQA to California's Housing Crisis," Holland & Knight, https://www.hklaw.com/en/case-studies/linking-ceqa-to-californias-housing-crisis.

20. Paul Groth, *Living Downtown: The History of Residential Hotels in the United States* (Berkeley: University of California Press, 1999), 92.

21. Ibid.

22. Ariel Aberg-Riger, "When America's Basic Housing Unit Was a Bed, Not a House," Bloomberg CityLab, last modified February 22, 2018, https://www.bloomberg.com/news/articles/2018-02-22/the-rise-and-fall-of-the-american-sro.

23. Ibid.

24. Ibid.

25. Ibid.

26. "Part 1: Point-in-Time Estimates of Homelessness," *The 2019 Annual Homeless Assessment Report* (AHAR) to Congress, 20.

27. Agis Salpukas, "Moratorium on Housing Subsidy Spells Hardship for Thousands," *The New York Times*, last modified April 16, 1973, https://www.nytimes.com/1973/04/16/archives/moratorium-onhousing-subsidy-spells-hardship-for-thousands-stricter.html.

28. William Tucker, "Cato Institute Policy Analysis No. 127: The Source of America's Housing Problem: Look in Your Own Back Yard," CATO Institute, February 6, 1990, https://www.cato.org/sites/cato.org/files/pubs/pdf/pa127.pdf.

29. Ibid.

30. David Wachsmuth, David Chaney, Danielle Kerrigan, Andrea Shillolo, and Robin Basalaev-Binder, *The High Cost of Short-Term Rentals in New York City*, Urban Politics and Governance research group, School of Urban Planning, McGill University, January 30, 2018, p. 35, https://www.mcgill.ca/newsroom/files/newsroom/channels/attach/airbnb-report.pdf.

31. Alastair Boone, "Airbnb Is Coming for Your Neighborhood," *Pacific Standard*, last modified March 12, 2018, https://psmag.com/economics/airbnb-is-coming-for-your-neighborhood.

32. "Investors are Buying Up Homes. Cincinnati is Pushing Back," *Wall Street*

Journal Podcasts, last modified January 27, 2022, https://www.wsj.com/
podcasts/the-journal/investors-are-buying-up-homes-cincinnati-is-pushing-back/
d98b7bec-2c9b-40cb-a693-cfa86c84092a.

33. Irina Ivanova, "After the crash: How Wall Street is driving up homelessness,"
CBS News, last modified February 26, 2019, https://www.cbsnews.com/news/
housing-crash-wall-street-homelessness-profits-over-people/.

34. *The State of the Nation's Housing 2020*, Joint Center for Housing Studies of Harvard
University, 1.

35. *The State of the Nation's Housing 2021*, Joint Center for Housing Studies of Harvard
University, 2020, p. 4, https://www.jchs.harvard.edu/sites/default/files/reports/
files/Harvard_JCHS_State_Nations_Housing_2021.pdf.

36. Ibid.

37. Michael Hyman, "April 2021 Existing-Home Sales Drop as Home Prices Rise and
Inventory Shortage Continues," National Association of Realtors, last modified
May 24, 2021, https://www.nar.realtor/blogs/economists-outlook/april-2021-ex-
isting-home-sales-drop-as-home-prices-rise-and-inventory-shortage-continues?utm_
source=dlvr.it&utm_medium=facebook.

38. Emily A. Shrider, Melissa Kollar, Frances Chen, and Jessica Semega, "Income and
Poverty in the United States: 2020," United States Census Bureau, last modified
September 14, 2021, https://www.census.gov/library/publications/2021/demo/
p60-273.html.

Chapter 8 - The Economy

1. "Labor Force Participation Rate – Women," U.S. Bureau of Labor Statistics, accessed
from FRED Economic Data, https://fred.stlouisfed.org/series/LNS11300002.

2. "Labor Force Participation Rate," U.S. Bureau of Labor Statistics, accessed from
FRED Economic Data, https://fred.stlouisfed.org/series/CIVPART.

3. "Employment Situation News Release," U.S. Bureau of Labor Statistics, last
modified February 2, 2018, https://www.bls.gov/news.release/archives/
empsit_02022018.htm.

4. *The Labor Force Participation Rate Since 2007: Causes and Policy Implications*,
The White House: President Barack Obama, July 2014, https://obamawhitehouse.
archives.gov/sites/default/files/docs/labor_force_participation_report.pdf.

5. Geoffrey C. Ho, Margaret Shih, Daniel J. Walters, and Todd L. Pittinsky, "The Stigma
of Unemployment: When joblessness leads to being jobless," UCLA: Institute for
Research on Labor and Employment, December 12, 2011, https://escholarship.
org/uc/item/7nh039h1#main.

6. Stan Alcorn, "'Check Yes Or No': The Hurdles Of Job Hunting With A
Criminal Past," NPR, last modified January 31, 2013, https://www.npr.

org/2013/01/31/170766202/-check-yes-or-no-the-hurdles-of-employment-with-criminal-past.

7. "Americans with Criminal Records," The Sentencing Project, https://www.sentencingproject.org/wp-content/uploads/2015/11/Americans-with-Criminal-Records-Poverty-and-Opportunity-Profile.pdf

8. Matthew Friedman, "Just Facts: As Many Americans Have Criminal Records as College Diplomas," Brennan Center for Justice, last modified November 17, 2015, https://www.brennancenter.org/our-work/analysis-opinion/just-facts-many-americans-have-criminal-records-college-diplomas.

9. Frederica Cocco, "Most US manufacturing jobs lost to technology, not trade," *Financial Times*, last modified December 2, 2016, https://www.ft.com/content/dec677c0-b7e6-11e6-ba85-95d1533d9a62.

10. James Manyika, Susan Lund, Michael Chui, Jacques Bughin, Jonathan Woetzel, Parul Batra, Ryan Ko, and Saurabh Sanghvi, "Jobs lost, jobs gained: What the future of work will mean for jobs, skills, and wages," McKinsey & Company, last modified November 28, 2017, https://www.mckinsey.com/featured-insights/future-of-work/jobs-lost-jobs-gained-what-the-future-of-work-will-mean-for-jobs-skills-and-wages.

11. Vernon Brundage, Jr., "Profile Of The Labor Force By Educational Attainment," U.S. Bureau of Labor Statistics, August 2017, p. 5, https://www.bls.gov/spotlight/2017/educational-attainment-of-the-labor-force/pdf/educational-attainment-of-the-labor-force.pdf.

12. Jay Shambaugh and Ryan Nunn, "Why Wages Aren't Growing in America," *Harvard Business Review*, last modified October 24, 2017, https://hbr.org/2017/10/why-wages-arent-growing-in-america.

13. Leslie Kramer, "What Is GDP and Why Is It So Important to Economists and Investors?", Investopedia, last modified January 31, 2022, https://www.investopedia.com/ask/answers/what-is-gdp-why-its-important-to-economists-investors/.

14. David Cooper and Lawrence Mishel, "The erosion of collective bargaining has widened the gap between productivity and pay," Economic Policy Institute, last modified January 6, 2015, https://www.epi.org/publication/collective-bargainings-erosion-expanded-the-productivity-pay-gap/.

15. Ibid.

16. Kathryn A. Edwards, "A $2.5 Trillion Question: What If Incomes Grew Like GDP Did?", Rand Corporation, last modified October 6, 2020, https://www.rand.org/blog/2020/10/a-25-trillion-question-what-if-incomes-grew-like-gdp.html.

17. Nick Hanauer and David M. Rolf, "The Top 1% of Americans Have Taken $50 Trillion From the Bottom 90%—And That's Made the U.S. Less Secure," *Time*, https://time.com/5888024/50-trillion-income-inequality-america/?utm_source=digg.

18. Kathryn A. Edwards, "A $2.5 Trillion Question."

19. Gerald Mayer, "Union membership Trends in the United States," Congressional Research Service, The Library of Congress, August 31, 2004, https://sgp.fas.org/crs/misc/RL32553.pdf.

20. "The real minimum wage," The FRED Blog, last modified July 23, 2015, https://fredblog.stlouisfed.org/2015/07/the-real-minimum-wage/.

21. Suresh Naidu, Eric Posner, and Glen Weyl, "More and more companies have monopoly power over workers' wages. That's killing the economy.", Vox, last modified April 6, 2018, https://www.vox.com/the-big-idea/2018/4/6/17204808/wages-employers-workers-monopsony-growth-stagnation-inequality.

22. Bob Pisani, "Stock buybacks surge to $850 billion in 2021, setting new record," CNBC, last modified December 30, 2021, https://www.cnbc.com/video/2021/12/30/2021-sees-850-billion-in-stock-buybacks-setting-new-record.html.

23. "QuickFacts: United States," United States Census Bureau, https://www.census.gov/quickfacts/fact/table/US/HSD410219.

24. Carter C. Price and Kathryn A. Edwards, "Trends in Income From 1975 to 2018," RAND Corporation, 2020, https://www.rand.org/pubs/working_papers/WRA516-1.html.

25. Michael Grover, "What a $400 emergency expense tells us about the economy," Federal Reserve Bank of Minneapolis, last modified June 11, 2021, https://www.minneapolisfed.org/article/2021/what-a-400-dollar-emergency-expense-tells-us-about-the-economy.

26. Heather Long, "How many Americans are unemployed? It's likely a lot more than 10 million," *The Washington Post*, last modified February 19, 2021, https://www.washingtonpost.com/business/2021/02/19/how-many-americans-unemployed/.

27. "5Y Price Chart" in "S&P 500 (^GSPC) Charts, Data and News," yahoo! Finance, https://finance.yahoo.com/quote/%5EGSPC/.

28. Quoctrung Bui, Kevin Quealy, and Rumsey Taylor, "Are You Rich? Where Does Your Net Worth Rank in America?", *The New York Times*, last modified August 12, 2019, https://www.nytimes.com/interactive/2019/08/12/upshot/are-you-rich-where-does-your-net-worth-rank-wealth.html.

29. Ben Steverman, "Harvard's Chetty Finds Economic Carnage in Wealthiest ZIP Codes," Bloomberg Businessweek, last modified September 24, 2020, https://www.bloomberg.com/news/features/2020-09-24/harvard-economist-raj-chetty-creates-god-s-eye-view-of-pandemic-damage.

Chapter 9 - Racism

1. "Race and Ethnicity in the United States: 2010 Census and 2020 Census," United States Census Bureau, last modified August 12, 2021, https://www.census.gov/library/visualizations/interactive/

race-and-ethnicity-in-the-united-state-2010-and-2020-census.html.

2. "Part 1: Point-in-Time Estimates of Homelessness," *The 2020 Annual Homeless Assessment Report (AHAR) to Congress*, The U.S. Department of Housing and Urban Development, January 2021, p. 8, https://www.huduser.gov/portal/sites/default/files/pdf/2020-AHAR-Part-1.pdf.

3. Dina Gerdeman, "Minorities Who 'Whiten' Job Resumes Get More Interviews," Harvard Business School, last modified May 17, 2017, https://hbswk.hbs.edu/item/minorities-who-whiten-job-resumes-get-more-interviews.

4. "Qualified Renters Need Not Apply: Study finds high levels of discrimination against Blacks, low-income renters," Suffolk University Boston, last modified June 26, 2020, https://www.suffolk.edu/news-features/news/2020/06/27/01/03/qualified-renters-need-not-apply.

5. David Oshinsky, "A Powerful, Disturbing History of Racial Segregation in America," *The New York Times*, last modified June 20, 2017, https://www.nytimes.com/2017/06/20/books/review/richard-rothstein-color-of-law-forgotten-history.html.

6. Richard Rothstein, *The Color of Law*, 54-55.

7. Jung Hyun Choi, "Breaking Down the Black-White Homeownership Gap," Urban Institute, last modified February 21, 2020, https://www.urban.org/urban-wire/breaking-down-black-white-homeownership-gap.

8. Richard Rothstein, *The Color of Law*, 111.

9. Kristin McIntosh, Emily Moss, Ryan Nunn, and Jay Shambaugh, "Examining the Black-white wealth gap," Brookings, last modified February 27, 2020, https://www.brookings.edu/blog/up-front/2020/02/27/examining-the-black-white-wealth-gap/.

10. Chris Hayes, *A Colony in a Nation* (New York: W. W. Norton & Company, 2017), 111.

11. "Report to the United Nations on Racial Disparities in the U.S. Criminal Justice System," The Sentencing Project, last modified April 19, 2018, https://www.sentencingproject.org/publications/un-report-on-racial-disparities/.

12. Ezekiel Edwards, Will Bunting, and Lynda Garcia, *The War on Marijuana in Black and White*, American Civil Liberties Union, June 2013, p. 4, https://www.aclu.org/files/assets/1114413-mj-report-rfs-rel1.pdf.

13. Charles M. Payne, "'The Whole United States Is Southern!': Brown v. Board and the Mystification of Race," *The Journal of American History* 91, no. 1 (2004): 83-91.

14. National Advisory Commission on Civil Disorders, *Report of the National Advisory Commission on Civil Disorders* (Washington, D.C.: United States Government Printing Office, 1968).

15. Ibid, 1.

16. Fred Harris, "The Unmet Promise of Equality," *The New York Times*, last modified

February 28, 2018, https://www.nytimes.com/interactive/2018/02/28/opinion/the-unmet-promise-of-equality.html.

Chapter 10 - Mental Illness

1. For sake of anonymity, I am not providing a direct citation for this quote. Everyone makes mistakes, and this person made a good faith effort to educate themselves and become part of the solution.

2. "Definition of Chronic Homelessness," HUD Exchange, https://www.hudexchange.info/homelessness-assistance/coc-esg-virtual-binders/coc-esg-homeless-eligibility/definition-of-chronic-homelessness/.

3. M. Jaross, Y. Kwak, & J. Gallant, *Marin County Homeless Count and Survey Comprehensive Report 2019*, 49-50.

4. Ibid.

5. "Mental Health Facts in America," National Alliance on Mental Illness, https://www.nami.org/nami/media/nami-media/infographics/generalmhfacts.pdf.

6. Ibid.

7. Ibid.

8. *Diagnostic and Statistical Manual of Mental Disorders*, Fifth ed., American Psychiatric Association, 2013, pp. 160-168, http://repository.poltekkes-kaltim.ac.id/657/1/Diagnostic%20and%20statistical%20manual%20of%20mental%20disorders%20_%20DSM-5%20%28%20PDFDrive.com%20%29.pdf.

9. "Does depression increase the risk for suicide?", U.S. Department of Health & Human Services, last modified September 16, 2014, https://www.hhs.gov/answers/mental-health-and-substance-abuse/does-depression-increase-risk-of-suicide/index.html#:~:text=The%20risk%20of%20death%20by,setting%20will%20die%20by%20suicide, and "Suicide," National Institute of Mental Health, https://www.nimh.nih.gov/health/statistics/suicide.

10. Jacob L. Stubbs, Allen E. Thornton, Jessica M. Sevick, Noah D. Silverberg, Alasdair M. Barr, William G. Honer, et. al., "Traumatic brain injury in homeless and marginally housed individuals: a systematic review and meta-analysis," *The Lancet* 5, no. 1 (2020): E19-E32.

11. "'I Tell What I Have Seen'—The Reports of Asylum Reformer Dorothea Dix," National Library of Medicine, last modified April 2006, https://www.ncbi.nlm.nih.gov/pmc/articles/PMC1470564/.

12. Matt Ford, "America's Largest Mental Hospital Is a Jail," *The Atlantic*, last modified June 8, 2015, https://www.theatlantic.com/politics/archive/2015/06/americas-largest-mental-hospital-is-a-jail/395012/.

13. John F. Kennedy, 1936, "Special Message to the Congress on Mental Illness and Mental Retardation.", Transcript of speech delivered at the White House, February

5, 1963, https://www.presidency.ucsb.edu/documents/special-message-the-congress-mental-illness-and-mental-retardation#:~:text=We%20must%20move%20from%20the,welfare%2C%20and%20legal%20protection%20services.

14. Ibid.

15. Matt Ford, "America's Largest Mental Hospital Is a Jail."

16. William Wan, "Pandemic relief bill delivers $4.25 billion for mental health services," *The Washington Post*, last modified December 21, 2020, https://www.washingtonpost.com/health/2020/12/21/mental-health-services-get-billions-relief-bill/.

17. Olga Khazan, "So You Think Someone Might Be Mentally Ill," *The Atlantic*, last modified February 16, 2018, https://www.theatlantic.com/health/archive/2018/02/so-you-think-someone-might-be-mentally-ill/553487/.

18. Stephanie Pellitt, "Trump Releases Budget Proposal, Seeks Medicaid Cuts and Opioid Funding," The National Council for Mental Wellbeing, last modified February 15, 2018, https://www.thenationalcouncil.org/capitol-connector/2018/02/trump-releases-budget-proposal-seeks-medicaid-cuts-opioid-funding/.

19. Stephen B. Seager, *Street Crazy: America's Mental Health Tragedy* (La Quinta: Westcom Associates, 2000), 131-133.

20. Ibid.

21. Richard D. Lyons, "How Release of Mental Health Patients Began," *The New York Times*, last modified October 30, 1984, https://www.nytimes.com/1984/10/30/science/how-release-of-mental-patients-began.html.

22. Matt Ford, "America's Largest Mental Hospital Is a Jail."

23. Ibid.

24. Elaine Dewees, "Legislation for the Mentally Ill," Los Angeles Times, last modified December 5, 1987, https://www.latimes.com/archives/la-xpm-1987-12-05-me-6108-story.html.

25. Matt Ford, "America's Largest Mental Hospital Is a Jail."

26. "Mental Health Treatment While Incarcerated," National Alliance on Mental Illness, https://www.nami.org/Advocacy/Policy-Priorities/Improving-Health/Mental-Health-Treatment-While-Incarcerated#:~:text=NAMI%20believes%20that%20all%20people,within%20prison%20and%20jail%20settings.

27. "Mental Illness: NAMI Report Deplores 80 Percent Unemployment Rate; State Rates and Ranks Listed—Model Legislation Proposed," National Alliance on Mental Illness, last modified January 1, 2014, https://www.nami.org/Press-Media/Press-Releases/2014/Mental-Illness-NAMI-Report-Deplores-80-Percent-Un-#:~:text=—One%20of%20the%20best%20steps,on%20Mental%20Illness%20(NAMI).

Chapter 11 - Addiction

1. "Biology of Addiction: Drugs and Alcohol Can Hijack Your Brain," News in Health, October 2015, https://newsinhealth.nih.gov/2015/10/biology-addiction.

2. Francesca Ducci and David Goldman, "The Genetic Basis of Addictive Disorders," *Psychiatric Clinics of North America* 35, no. 2 (2012): 495-519.

3. Gabor Maté, *In the Realm of Hungry Ghosts: Close Encounters with Addiction* (Berkeley: North Atlantic Books, 2010).

4. Len Kelly, Book Review of *In the Realm of Hungry Ghosts: Close Encounters with Addiction* by Gabor Maté, in *Can Fam Physician* 54, no. 6 (2008), 894.

5. Gabor Maté, interview by Tim Ferriss, *The Tim Ferriss Show*, June 4, 2018, https://tim.blog/2018/06/04/the-tim-ferriss-show-transcripts-dr-gabor-mate/.

6. Gerald Deneau, Tomoji Yanagita, and M. H. Seevers, "Self-Administration of Psychoactive Substances by the Monkey: A Measure of Psychological Dependence," *Psychopharmacologia* 16 (1969).

7. Johann Hari, *Chasing the Scream: The Opposite of Addiction is Connection* (London: Bloomsbury, 2016), 172.

8. Ibid., 173.

9. Alexandre Tanzi, "U.S. Had Most Drug Overdose Deaths on Record in 2020, CDC Says," Bloomberg, last modified July 14, 2021, https://www.bloomberg.com/news/articles/2021-07-14/u-s-had-most-drug-overdose-deaths-on-record-in-2020-cdc-says.

10. "Drug Overdose Deaths in the U.S. Top 100,000 Annually," Centers for Disease Control and Prevention, last modified November 17, 2021, https://www.cdc.gov/nchs/pressroom/nchs_press_releases/2021/20211117.htm.

11. Alex Hollingsworth, Christopher J. Ruhm, & Kosali Simon, "Macroeconomic Conditions and Opioid Abuse," National Bureau of Economic Research, last modified March 2017, https://www.nber.org/papers/w23192.

12. Nadine Burke Harris, *The Deepest Well: Healing the Long-Term Effects of Childhood Trauma and Adversity* (Boston: Mariner Books, 2021), 37.

13. Ibid., 38.

14. Ibid.

15. Ibid.

16. Ibid., 70.

17. Vincent J. Felitti, "The Origins of Addiction: Evidence from the Adverse Childhood Experiences Study," Department of Preventive Medicine, Kaiser Permanente Medical Care Program, last modified December 28, 2003, p. 7, https://www.nijc.org/pdfs/Subject%20Matter%20Articles/Drugs%20and%20Alc/ACE%20Study%20-%20OriginsofAddiction.pdf.

18. Gabor Maté, *In the Realm of Hungry Ghosts: Close Encounters with Addiction*, 37.

Chapter 12 - The Modern Homelessness Crisis

1. *The State of the Nation's Housing 2018*, Joint Center for Housing Studies of Harvard University, 2018, p. 5, https://www.jchs.harvard.edu/sites/default/files/Harvard_JCHS_State_of_the_Nations_Housing_2018.pdf.

2. Daniel Kim, *Introduction to Systems Thinking* (Arcadia: Pegasus Communications, 1999), https://thesystemsthinker.com/introduction-to-systems-thinking/.

Chapter 13 - A Predictable Response

1. Lucio Villa, Benjamin Din, and Emma O'Neill, "How 5 mayors tackled homelessness," *San Francisco Chronicle*, last modified June 26, 2016, https://projects.sfchronicle.com/sf-homeless/letters-from-the-mayors/.

2. Elisabeth Kübler-Ross, *On Death and Dying* (New York: The MacMillan Company, 1969).

3. Ibid.

4. Ibid.

5. Lucio Villa, Benjamin Din, and Emma O'Neill, "How 5 mayors tackled homelessness."

6. Ibid.

7. Ibid.

8. Rebecca Cohen, Will Yetvin, and Jill Khadduri, *Understanding Encampments of People Experiencing Homelessness and Community Responses*, U.S. Department of Housing and Urban Development, January 7, 2019, https://www.huduser.gov/portal/sites/default/files/pdf/Understanding-Encampments.pdf.

9. Ibid.

10. "Part 1: Point-in-Time Estimates of Homelessness," *The 2019 Annual Homeless Assessment Report* (AHAR) to Congress, 13.

11. Anna Gorman and Kaiser Health News, "Medieval Diseases Are Infecting California's Homeless," *The Atlantic*, last modified March 8, 2019, https://www.theatlantic.com/health/archive/2019/03/typhus-tuberculosis-medieval-diseases-spreading-homeless/584380/.

12. Adam McGill, "Marin Voice: Police bear increasingly heavy burden of society's problems," *Marin Independent Journal*, last modified December 30, 2018, https://www.marinij.com/2018/12/30/marin-voice-police-bear-increasingly-heavy-burden-of-societys-problems/.

13. Lucio Villa, Benjamin Din, and Emma O'Neill, "How 5 mayors tackled homelessness."

Illustrations

1. Genaro Molina, *Police Visiting an Encampment in Los Angeles*, Licensed Photograph,

Los Angeles Times, Polaris.

2. Al Seib, *Clearing an Encampment in Los Angeles*, Licensed Photograph, Los Angeles Times, Polaris.

Chapter 14 - The Homeless Industrial Complex

1. "Transcript of President Dwight D. Eisenhower's Farewell Address (1961)," ourdocuments.gov, https://www.ourdocuments.gov/doc.php?flash=false&doc=90&page=transcript.

2. "Industrial complex," Wikipedia, last modified February 15, 2022, https://en.wikipedia.org/wiki/Industrial_complex.

3. Donella H. Meadows, *Thinking in Systems*, 112.

4. I determined this by accessing databases such as https://sfserviceguide.org/, https://www.1degree.org/, and https://www.211bayarea.org/.

5. Laura Kurtzman, "Study Finds Permanent Supportive Housing is Effective for Highest Risk Chronically Homeless People," University of California San Francisco, last modified September 17, 2020, https://www.ucsf.edu/news/2020/09/418546/study-finds-permanent-supportive-housing-effective-highest-risk-chronically.

Chapter 15 - Rationalizing Inaction

1. M. Jaross, Y. Kwak, & J. Gallant, *Marin County Homeless Count and Survey Comprehensive Report 2019*, 12.

2. W. F. Lloyd, *Two Lectures on the Checks to Population* (Oxford: Oxford University Press, 1833).

3. *Santa Clara County Homeless Census & Survey Comprehensive Report 2019*, Applied Survey Research, 2019, p. 8, https://osh.sccgov.org/sites/g/files/exjcpb671/files/2019%20SCC%20Homeless%20Census%20and%20Survey%20Report.pdf;*San Francisco Homeless Count & Survey 2019 Executive Summary*, Applied Survey Research, 2019, https://hsh.sfgov.org/wp-content/uploads/2020/01/Executive-Summary_SanFrancisco2019.pdf; *Marin County Homeless Count & Survey 2019 Executive Summary*, Applied Survey Research, 2019, https://www.marinhhs.org/sites/default/files/files/servicepages/2019_07/executivesummary_marin2019.pdf; "Continuum of Care," County of Sonoma, https://sonomacounty.ca.gov/development-services/community-development-commission/divisions/homeless-services/continuum-of-care; *Solano County Homeless Count & Survey 2019 Executive Summary*, Applied Survey Research, 2019, https://nebula.wsimg.com/e464819ebca2a5fd1a08032dec6aa038?AccessKeyId=B6ADA8353DCF8737BDC0&disposition=0&alloworigin=1; *Alameda County 2019 EveryOne Counts Homeless*

Point-in-Time Count & Survey, Applied Survey Research, 2019, https://everyone-home.org/wp-content/uploads/2019/07/ExecutiveSummary_Alameda2019-1. pdf; *Santa Cruz County Homeless Census & Survey 2019 Executive Summary, Applied Survey Research*, 2019, https://housingmatterssc.org/wp-content/ uploads/2019/08/2019-PIT-Count-Exec-Summary.pdf.

4. "Acting to Prevent, Reduce and End Homelessness," Homeless Data Integration System, State of California Business, Consumer Services and Housing Agency, https://bcsh.ca.gov/calich/hdis.html.

5. Kevin Fagan and Lea Suzuki, "Seven lives, seven paths, little change seen," *San Francisco Chronicle*, last modified December 2016, https://projects.sfchronicle. com/sf-homeless/division-street-map/.

Chapter 16 - Hitting Rock Bottom in Marin

1. U.S. News Staff, "The 15 Richest Counties in the U.S.," U.S. News, last modified December 11, 2020, https://www.usnews.com/news/healthiest-communities/ slideshows/richest-counties-in-america?slide=3.

2. Lynda Roberts, "November 3, 2020 Presidential General Election," County of Marin, https://www.marincounty.org/depts/rv/election-info/past-elections/page-data/ tabs-collection/past2020/nov-3.

3. "The Bay and Protected Open Space," Marin Convention and Visitors Bureau, https://www.visitmarin.org/things-to-do/outdoor-activities/ the-bay-and-protected-open-space/.

4. J. K. Dineen, "Here's why Marin continues to be the Bay Area's most segregated county," *San Francisco Chronicle*, last modified December 8, 2020, https:// www.sfchronicle.com/bayarea/article/Restrictive-zoning-keeps-Marin-the-most-15782840.php.

5. "Housing Need," California Housing Partnership, https://chpc.net/housingneed s/?view=37.405074,-119.26758,5&county=California,Marin&group=housing-need&chart=shortfall%7Ccurrent,cost-burden%7Ccurrent,cost-burden-re%7Ccur-rent,homelessness,historical-rents,vacancy,asking-rents%7C2021,budgets%7C2021,-funding%7Ccurrent,state-funding,lihtc%7C2010:2020:historical,rhna-progress,mul-tifamily-production.

6. M. Jaross, Y. Kwak, & J. Gallant, *Marin County Homeless Count and Survey Comprehensive Report 2019, Applied Survey Research*, 14.

7. Jill Tucker and Emma Talley, "Two Marin schools forced to integrate after years of segregation and battles for funding," *San Francisco Chronicle*, last modified June 18, 2021, https://www.sfchronicle.com/education/article/Two-Marin-schools-forced-to-integrate-after-years-16256418.php#photo-21138763.

8. Jeremiah Mock, "Trends in Youth Alcohol, Cannabis and Other Drug Use in Marin

232

County, 2008-18," Marin Health and Human Services, October 7, 2020, p. 4, https://www.marinhhs.org/sites/default/files/files/servicepages/2020_11/marin_county_trends_in_youth_alcohol_cannabis_and_other_drug_use_2008-18_100720jm.pdf.

9. Michele Berrong, A. J. Brady, Julie Michaels, Christine O'Hanlon, Rob Reinhard, Kim Turner, and Mark Vanderscoff, *Marin Chronic Alcohol with Justice Involvement Project BUSINESS PLAN – JUNE 2013*, County of Marin, June 4, 2013, p. 3, https://www.marinhhs.org/sites/default/files/rfp/2015/marin_caji_project_bp_pdf_-_6-4-13.pdf.

10. Ibid.

Chapter 17 - The Most Visible and Vulnerable

1. Author's recollection of internal data collecting efforts of the City of San Rafael from approximately 2017 to 2019.

2. Ibid.

3. Malcolm Gladwell, "Million-Dollar Murray," *The New Yorker*, last modified February 5, 2006, https://www.newyorker.com/magazine/2006/02/13/million-dollar-murray.

4. Seiji Hayashi, "How Health and Homelessness are Connected—Medically," *The Atlantic*, last modified January 25, 2016, https://www.theatlantic.com/politics/archive/2016/01/how-health-and-homelessness-are-connectedmedically/458871/.

Chapter 19 - Housing First

1. Robert M. Pirsig, *Zen and the Art of Motorcycle Maintenance* (New York: Harper-Collins, 2008), as cited in Donella Meadows, Thinking in Systems, XV.

2. Author's recollection from a presentation by Iain De Jong in Spring 2018, Marin County, CA.

3. Laura Kurtzman, "Study Finds Permanent Supportive Housing is Effective for Highest Risk Chronically Homeless People," and Philip W. Appel, Sam Tsemberis, Herman Joseph, Ana Stefancic, and Dawn Lambert-Wacey, "Housing first for severely mentally ill homeless methadone patients," J Addict Dis. 31 no. 3 (2012), 270-277.

Chapter 20 - Coordinated Entry

1. "Coordinated Entry Fact Sheet," United States Department of Veterans Affairs, last modified February 2018, https://www.va.gov/HOMELESS/ssvf/docs/VA_Coordinated_Entry_Fact_Sheet_February2018_Final.pdf.

2. "History – 2004," "Who We Are," Breaking Ground, https://breakingground.org/who-we-are/.

3. Josh Leopold and Helen Ho, *Evaluation of the 100,000 Homes Campaign*, Urban Institute, last modified February 2015, p. 11, https://www.urban.org/sites/default/files/publication/44391/2000148-Evaluation-of-the-100000-Homes-Campaign.pdf.

4. "100,000 Homes Campaign: A Success Story," Substance Abuse and Mental Health Services Administration, last modified August 4, 2016, https://www.samhsa.gov/homelessness-programs-resources/hpr-resources/100000-homes-campaign.

5. Josh Leopold and Helen Ho, *Evaluation of the 100,000 Homes Campaign*, 2.

6. "Built for Zero," MeasureD, https://measured.design/built-for-zero/.

7. *Getting to Proof Points*, Community Solutions, last modified March 2018, pp. 3-4, https://community.solutions/wp-content/uploads/2019/10/bfz_impact_report_-_final.pdf.

8. *Built for Zero Canada Functional Zero Homelessness Question and Answer Document*, Built for Zero Canada, last modified February 11, 2021, p. 2, https://bfzcanada.ca/wp-content/uploads/Functional-Zero-QA.pdf.

9. Nuala Bishari, "In San Francisco, Hundreds of Homes for the Homeless Sit Vacant," ProPublica, last modified February 24, 2022, https://www.propublica.org/article/in-san-francisco-hundreds-of-homes-for-the-homeless-sit-vacant.

10. "Monthly Stats for February 2022," Homelessness in Marin, last modified February 2022, https://housingfirst.marinhhs.org/data-dashboard.

11. "Built for Zero," Community Solutions, https://community.solutions/built-for-zero/.

Chapter 21 - Bringing It All Together

1. "Part 1: Point-in-Time Estimates of Homelessness," *The 2019 Annual Homeless Assessment Report (AHAR) to Congress*, 13.

2. Ibid., 12.

3. *Marin County Homeless Count and Survey Executive Summary 2017, Applied Survey Research*, Marin Health and Human Services, https://www.marinhhs.org/sites/default/files/files/servicepages/2017_07/marin_pit_executive_summary_2017.pdf.

Chapter 22 - Fixes That Fail

1. "Fixes that fail," Wikipedia, last modified January 22, 2022, https://en.wikipedia.org/wiki/Fixes_that_fail.

2. "Economic Mobility: Measuring the American Dream," PD&R Edge, https://www.huduser.gov/portal/pdredge/pdr_edge_featd_article_071414.html.

3. Laura Sullivan and Meg Anderson, "Section 8 Vouchers Help The Poor — But Only If Housing Is Available," NPR, last modified May 10, 2017, https://www.npr.org/2017/05/10/527660512/

section-8-vouchers-help-the-poor-but-only-if-housing-is-available.

4. Andrew Woo, "Imbalance in Housing Aid," Apartment List, last modified October 11, 2017, https://www.apartmentlist.com/research/imbalance-housing-aid-mortgage-interest-deduction-vs-section-8.

5. "Marin County California Residential Rent and Rental Statistics," Department of Numbers, https://www.deptofnumbers.com/rent/california/marin-county/.

6. Thomas Piketty, *Capital in the 21st Century*, trans. Arthur Goldhammer (Cambridge, MA: Belknap Press, 2017).

7. Ibid.

8. Ibid.

9. Matthew Desmond, "How Home Ownership Became the Engine of American Inequality," *The New York Times*, last modified May 9, 2017, https://www.nytimes.com/2017/05/09/magazine/how-homeownership-became-the-engine-of-american-inequality.html.

10. Matthew Desmond, *Evicted: Poverty and Profit in the American City* (Crown: New York, 2017), 306.

Chapter 23 - The Big Eight

1. Mark P. Cussen, "Top 5 Reasons Why People Go Bankrupt," Investopedia, last modified February 19, 2022, https://www.investopedia.com/financial-edge/0310/top-5-reasons-people-go-bankrupt.aspx.

2. Daniel Kim, *Introduction to Systems Thinking* (Arcadia: Pegasus Communications, 1999), p. 5, https://thesystemsthinker.com/introduction-to-systems-thinking/.

3. Lea Lane, "Percentage Of Americans Who Never Traveled Beyond The State Where They Were Born? A Surprise," Forbes, last modified May 2, 2019, https://www.forbes.com/sites/lealane/2019/05/02/percentage-of-americans-who-never-traveled-beyond-the-state-where-they-were-born-a-surprise/?sh=4d1629152898.

4. Courtney Martin, "The Reductive Seduction of Other People's Problems," BRIGHT Magazine, last modified January 11, 2016, https://brightthemag.com/the-reductive-seduction-of-other-people-s-problems-3c07b307732d.

5. Mauricio L. Miller, *The Alternative: Most of What You Believe about Poverty Is Wrong* (self-published: Lulu Press, 2017), 31-32.

6. "California's High Housing Costs: Causes and Consequences," Legislative Analyst's Office, last modified March 17, 2015, https://lao.ca.gov/reports/2015/finance/housing-costs/housing-costs.aspx.

7. Jonathan Woetzel, Jan Mischke, Shannon Peloquin, and Daniel Weisfield, *A Tool Kit to Close California's Housing Gap: 3.5 Million Homes By 2025*, McKinsey Global Institute, McKinsey & Company, October 2016, https://www.mckinsey.com/~/

media/mckinsey/industries/public%20and%20social%20sector/our%20insights/
closing%20californias%20housing%20gap/closing-californias-housing-gap-full-re-
port.pdf.

8. "The Cost of Building Housing Series," Terner Center, last modified March 20,
2020, https://ternercenter.berkeley.edu/research-and-policy/the-cost-of-build-
ing-housing-series/#:~:text=Affordable%20Housing%20Costs%3A%20The%20
cost,and%20regulation.

9. Ben Metcalf, David Garcia, Ian Carlton, and Kate McFarlane, *Will Allowing Duplexes
and Lot Splits on Parcels Zoned for Single-Family Create New Homes?: Assessing the
Viability of New Housing Supply Under California's Senate Bill 9*, Terner Center,
July 2021, p. 8, https://ternercenter.berkeley.edu/wp-content/uploads/2021/07/
SB-9-Brief-July-2021-Final.pdf.

10. Rutger Bregman, "The bizarre tale of President Nixon and his basic income bill," The
Correspondent, last modified May 17, 2016, https://thecorrespondent.com/4503/
the-bizarre-tale-of-president-nixon-and-his-basic-income-bill/173117835-c34d6145.

11. Ibid.

12. Kristin McIntosh, Emily Moss, Ryan Nunn, and Jay Shambaugh, "Examining the
Black-white wealth gap."

13. Jeffrey Olivet, Marc Dones, Molly Richard, Catriona Wilkey, Svetlana, Yampolskaya,
Maya Beit-Arie, and Lunise Joseph, *SPARC: Supporting Partnerships for Anti-Racist
Communities: Phase One Study Findings*, Center for Social Innovation, March 2018,
https://c4innovates.com/wp-content/uploads/2019/03/SPARC-Phase-1-Findings-
March-2018.pdf.

14. "Anosognosia," National Alliance on Mental Illness, https://www.nami.org/
About-Mental-Illness/Common-with-Mental-Illness/Anosognosia#:~:tex-
t=800%2D950%2DNAMI&text=When%20someone%20rejects%20a%20
diagnosis,enough%20to%20consciously%20choose%20denial.

15. Sam Quinones, "I Don't Know That I Would Even Call It Meth Anymore," *The
Atlantic*, last modified October 18, 2021, https://www.theatlantic.com/magazine/
archive/2021/11/the-new-meth/620174/.

16. Heather Knight, "Castro woman known for wandering into traffic is dead. Why
couldn't S.F. save her?", *San Francisco Chronicle*, last modified December 7, 2020,
https://www.sfchronicle.com/bayarea/heatherknight/article/Castro-homeless-
woman-known-for-wandering-into-15783160.php.

Epilogue

1. Donella H. Meadows, *Thinking in Systems*, 4.

Made in the USA
Las Vegas, NV
06 December 2023

82202522R00136